LIFE GOES BETTER *with* CHOCOLATE GRAVY

MOUNTAIN MEMORIES—MISCHIEF *and* MISERY

NORMA PATRICK SETO

WESTBOW
PRESS®
A DIVISION OF THOMAS NELSON
& ZONDERVAN

WestBow Press books may be ordered through booksellers or by contacting:

WestBow Press
A Division of Thomas Nelson & Zondervan
1663 Liberty Drive
Bloomington, IN 47403
www.westbowpress.com
844-714-3454

Bible scripture from the King James Version of the Bible.

ISBN: 978-1-6642-1333-3 (sc)
ISBN: 978-1-6642-1335-7 (hc)
ISBN: 978-1-6642-1334-0 (e)

Library of Congress Control Number: 2020923134

Print information available on the last page.

WestBow Press rev. date: 12/10/2020

Dedicated to Maxine Crase Patrick.

Recorded with much love for Bethany, Rob, and Nathanial Mueller; Kelly, Jeffrey, Jared, and Perry and Whitney Neal; Matthew, Patty, Hero, and Max Seto; Juanita and Gary Richter; Dennis, Nancy, and Ian Richter; Diane, Blaine, Nicholas, Sydney, Taylor Maxine, Bailey, and Lilianna Bacher; Debbie, Clay, Mason, and Elianna Rettig; and Dale McCoy Richter.

In loving memory of McCoy Patrick, Vencin Patrick, Juanita Patrick Richter, Andy and Lucy Belle Elam Crase, Fairsh and Lizzie McGuire Patrick.

In appreciation of the late Nina K. Brown Flynt, English teacher, Salyersville High School.

NORMA PATRICK SETO In this book, Norma Patrick Seto paints pictures with words. Words of legends, of mysteries, and of histories. Broad strokes of bright paint will allow your mind to feast on colorful stories. Folklore often gets lost over the ages. Norma documents much folklore with the telling of incidents shared by elders, memories of situations in her own home, growing up as a child. She does this in the way a grandmother might share a family story as she gently rocks a nodding head who desires to hear more, and strains to stay awake to that end. The stories unravel as if from a favorite uncle willing to enlighten his next of kin with ramblings that may be hard to believe…but which did in fact happen. Many of these stories are hard to believe, and by sharing, she reveals the hardships of a steely strong people – of people who survived in the most challenging of times. She shows the curiosity which people had to have in order to find relief in some of the maladies they faced. She shares happy stories, fun stories and sad stories, and like the story the uncle is sharing, one never knows what is coming next. I have had the distinct pleasure of knowing Norma since we were eighth graders. Through many years, we have been best friends and a great support to each other. We grew up in the same area of Kentucky and thus shared many of the peculiarities of the place and the people. I mean this in the sweetest most sincere of ways, for she and I both are grateful for our beginnings, for the families we each had, for the teachers who offered encouragement, for our friends and neighbors and for the values we learned from all of those around us. We discuss these gifts often. One of the greatest gifts a friend can offer another, is to believe in them, give them confidence, to support them when they are weak – she has been all that and more for me. She is a true friend. Norma shared many of her stories in this book with me through the years. We broke the routine of our lives to pen stories we each wanted to share on "writing getaways". Her stories are most interesting because they are all based on real people, real life situations, personal beliefs, and real-life pain and suffering. She retells stories which reveal solutions to situations or conditions which may appear unbelievable. And though I doubted some of the customs or 'beliefs' practiced and revealed herein, specifically pertaining to certain water which was 100% bacteria free and used in certain healing situations, I dove into a modern-day source and confirmed it is, in fact, true. The reader will find sheer enjoyment in her style of presentation. Right to the point, interjections of comments as to customs and again legends, mysteries and histories.

Dolly Kohls, friend of Norma Patrick Seto since 1958!

Through her heartwarming, humorous, and entertaining memoir of growing up in the hills of eastern Kentucky, Norma invites us to meet colorful characters who lived life the way it was meant to be lived – simply and to the fullest.

Dr. Jeffrey F. Neal, Director, Cooperative Education Program
Clemson University, Center for Career and Professional Development

CONTENTS

INTRODUCTION

People from eastern Kentucky are smart, creative, talented, and good-looking.

I am proud of my heritage.

While recorded history might be accurate and informative, the simple, funny, actual events and attitudes are sometimes lost to the record as generations die off. My desire is to record for my own family and others the incidents, stories, sense of humor, certain beliefs, survival, neighboring, and child-rearing that give flavor to our history. If some of my writing offends, just be aware that we have come a long way in how we now live—some good ways and maybe some not-so-good ways.

All the stories recorded here are true and not intended to undermine anyone or any way of life. I wrote to convey a slice of life mostly during the 1940s, '50s, and '60s. The people and circumstances you will read about helped to shape my life, lay the groundwork for good work ethic, nurture and build a strong faith in God, and give me an appreciation for the simple things. I believe that what I experienced growing up positively impacted my own life and the lives of my children.

These experiences were not the same for everyone. Within the small communities on Johnson Fork, there were people who lived comfortably and those who struggled to get by and get a start in life. My family struggled. People who lived and grew up in the small town of Salyersville, our county seat, might find some of these stories as far-fetched as someone who lived in a big city far away.

FIRST MEMORIES

The plunder (household furniture) was piled high on the bed of a mule-drawn wagon. The rockers of my small red chair turned upside down on the top made a fitting crown for all the worldly goods my family owned.

We had moved from Turkey Branch to the Jesse Williams Farm on Johnson Fork to Long Branch and, with this move, back to Turkey Branch.

When Mom and Dad had an opportunity to rent or sharecrop a small farm, we simply moved, and a dwelling place was part of the package. No money changed hands. A place to live and a portion of the crops were exchanged for all the hard work it took to run a small farm. The agreement was sealed with an honest man's word and a handshake.

In the early days, none of the houses we lived in had indoor plumbing or electricity. An open grate fireplace or woodburning stove provided heat but seldom warmed more than just a portion of one room. I remember on occasion waking up thirsty and going to the kitchen for a drink of water, only to find the dipper frozen solid in a bucket of ice.

THE TESTIMONY

Just a few years ago, I was asked to be part of a large effort to generate interest and spark enthusiasm for a building program at church. Each individual involved was asked at some point to give a personal testimony in front of the congregation. I was not a public speaker, and what's more, I had a very simple testimony: a simple sinner saved by God's grace. I was raised in a Christian family, and at that point, I'd had no traumatic events in my life from which to build an impressive personal story. I had been blessed with good health and surrounded by people who nurtured and loved me.

I labored over the content of the personal testimony until I remembered a very small task that I was asked to perform for the Mount Zion Baptist Church on Johnson Fork in Magoffin County, Kentucky. I was twelve years old. I am now seventy-six.

Built in the late 1800s, the church building consists of one large room with three windows on each side and two windows at the back behind the pulpit. From the turn of the century to the present, two doors at the front have welcomed generations of honest, hardworking, God-fearing folks to worship and fellowship. I don't know why in the beginning two doors were installed at the front of a relatively small one-room meeting house. The left door was used by the women and the door on the right side was used by the men. The men actually sat on the right side of the church, and the women sat on the left. No written or verbal rule applied for separating the men and women; that was just the way it worked. Children usually sat with their parents, or they sat in the middle section, where Mom, Dad, or a grandparent could keep a watchful eye.

In winter, the church was heated by a potbellied stove. A member who lived near the church would arrive well ahead of schedule to build a fire. The same person usually brought a bucket of water drawn from his own well. The bucket sat on a table near the pulpit. A long- handled dipper floated on the top and served as a drinking vessel for any and all who needed a drink of water. Even back then I wondered at the wisdom of everyone drinking from the same dipper. I had to be extremely thirsty to get a drink for myself, especially when I watched a man hold the dipper to his mouth as water mixed with tobacco spittle ran down the sides of his mouth and dropped from his chin to the floor.

Toilets were outside and to the left of the church building, separated by just enough space for several horses to be hitched. The human smells blended with the smells the horses created. Similarly, the sounds of the horses blended with the sounds of song, preaching, and praise coming from inside the church. The memory of stomping hooves, swishing tails, and a mountain rendition of "Amazing Grace" brings into focus a rich heritage that grounds me and gives me joy.

Which brings me to the task I was asked to perform.

I was asked to paint two small signs to mark the men's and the women's toilets. Starting with two unpainted boards of similar size, I painted large black block letters on a white background. It was a simple service done many years ago, yet as I drive by the church today, I see the signs are still there.

The church is freshly painted but otherwise unchanged. The toilets remain unpainted but fully functional one-holers with clear signs over each door, painted in my own hand so long ago, helping my friends make their way to meet a basic human need.

As I shared this story with the modern-day congregation of my Ohio church, I summed up my testimony with these remarks:

> It is the simple things you do along the way to point people in the right direction that makes a *lasting* difference in the long run.

I confess I wanted and expected the laughter that followed. I do not intend to make light of a serious responsibility to share the good news of God's love. I believe that God's plan for us is very simple. We sometimes complicate it with our own high ideas, traditions, and rituals. I do believe that there is absolute truth. There is a God who loves us. Our sinful nature creates a gap between him and us. But in his love and mercy, he has made a way for us to bridge that gap and have fellowship through his Son, Jesus Christ.

This story was written and this photo was taken of the women's toilet before it was torn down.

NORMA PATRICK SETO

MEMORABLE MOVE

The wagon rolled slowly down the proach (approach) and into the creek. The mules stopped to take a long drink of water before they continued on the journey that led to the mouth of Long Branch, past Ed Burton's store, and down Johnson Fork. The mules had two miles of easy pulling before we reached the mouth of Turkey Branch. From there it was slow moving through a narrow creek bed and up a small hill to the cabin where I was born just five years earlier.

Sharecroppers are apt to move often and sometimes return to farms they have tended in years past.

A few feet from where the mules stopped to drink, there was a small pool of water, cool and still and partly hidden by the fern-draped bank, away from the current that wandered from the head of Long Branch.

Once when Dad came home from a long day's work, he spoke of a surprise waiting for us at the creek. The only condition was that we must eat supper before we could retrieve it. When supper was finally over and the dishes were done, my sister and I ran barefoot to the creek to discover four bottles of soda pop cooling in the pool of water. That was my very first taste of bottled pop.

Juanita and Normalene Patrick and our dog, Crickett.
Taken in front of our home on Long Branch.

Maxine Crase Patrick. Taken by the well box at home on Long
Branch. She was about twenty-eight years old at the time.

A MATCH MADE

They met at church. She decided against him at first because he was poorly groomed and shabbily dressed. When Maxine turned down Coy's offer to walk her home, he determined to look more appealing when next he saw her. Meanwhile, she and her sisters made light of the boy who had shown interest. When Coy decided to visit her home the next week, he arrived on a fine horse. He wore a starched white shirt, his shoes were well shined, and his black hair was oiled and combed back straight with just a strand falling over his forehead. "He's mine!" Maxine said, and the rest is history. The following paragraphs record the humble beginnings of an interesting journey through life for my parents, Maxine Crase Patrick and McCoy (Coy) Patrick.

They were married on March 6, 1940. He turned twenty on June 29, and she turned twenty on August 5 of the same year. Lura Davis and Jim Rudd "stood up with them," which means they witnessed the ceremony and signed the marriage certificate.

The simple ceremony was at the bride's home with her dad, Andy Crase, reluctantly officiating. He remarked to Coy, "You'll have her back here in a week." She had always been high-spirited and independent.

For very good reasons, their plans to marry were kept secret from most of their friends and family. The mischievous custom of chivaree was very common at the time and in that place. What should be a happy occasion could easily turn into a nightmare for the bride and groom. Folks who were normally very loving and supportive might get caught up in the tradition of playing pranks on a newly-wed couple.

Just a week before the marriage of Coy and Maxine, their friends Hack and Olive Waters were wed. News of the ceremony leaked and spread. The groom suffered the pain and embarrassment of being ridden astraddle a rough section of split rail fence. He was carried by two men on each end of the rail until they reached the creek and was then dunked into the icy cold February creek water. The bride was humiliated when firecrackers were thrown up her dress and cowbells were tied to the marriage bed springs.

Pranks were limited only by the participants' creativity.

When a couple decided to get married, they sought out a preacher and asked a couple of witnesses to stand up with them, which was no less than the law required for signing the certificate. Of course, the bride and groom wore their best clothes and shoes, but no guests or other preparations were planned or expected.

When Coy and Maxine arrived at his parents' home after the ceremony that evening, Lizzie had made chicken and dumplings for the wedding supper. A few friends came to eat and wish them well. Frank and Ruth Reed came with their daughters, Virginia and Phyllis. Jim and Lola Reed were there with their children, Maxine and Elwood. Bert and Judy Reed, who were general store owners, came and brought a pink glass platter for the newly married couple.

Coy's brother, Logan, and his wife, Tressie, came with their children, Arthur, Myrtle, and Junior. The children of Logan and Tressie were friendly and flirtatious with Maxine, and she remembers that they showed their affection by slapping her and spitting on her.

Singles in attendance were Savannah (Maxine's sister), Lura Davis (Maxine's cousin), Delmar Elam (the groom's nephew), and Vencin Patrick (Coy's brother).

Coy and Maxine lived with his parents, Fairsh and Lizzie Patrick, for three weeks and then moved to a primitive two-room house farther up Settlement Branch. Previous residents had conveniently left a woodburning cookstove, a round table, and a rocking chair. The chair had one good rocker and one broken rocker. Coy used a tobacco stick to make a rocker that worked well enough to make the chair usable.

The walls and floors were far from airtight. Maxine stuffed rags in the spaces between boards and then papered over them with what she called building paper. Through cracks in the floor, they could watch the chickens moving about under the house.

To quote Maxine: "We were as happy as could be."

Note: I shared this story with a friend who was born and bred in New York. He had never heard of a tobacco stick and asked for an explanation. This is for anyone who might be just as curious.

Every tobacco grower in the area had their own good supply (hundreds) of tobacco sticks roughly cut from the nearby woods and shaped to a point at both ends. When tobacco was harvested in late summer, the wooden sticks were hauled by sled or wagon into the field. One end of a wooden tobacco stick was shoved into the ground, and a metal spear was placed over the upper end. As the stalks of tobacco were cut, they were speared onto the stick, which held about eight to ten large tobacco plants. The metal spear was moved to the next wooden stick, and the action was repeated until all the green tobacco plants were cut and speared. The full sticks were hauled into the barn and hung over the rafters to dry.

The next step toward getting it ready for market happened when the tobacco had turned brown. Because the plants were too dry to handle at that point, the farmer had to wait for rain, which brought humidity. I can remember Dad lighting his kerosene lantern and going in the middle of the night to the barn to check if the tobacco was "in case." If he found it just right to handle, he then enlisted the help of others to book the tobacco. Booking involved taking the plants from the rafters, stacking them, and covering them well to hold in the dampness.

The task of stripping the tobacco could now begin. One or two persons were given the job of stripping, or tearing, the leaves from the stalks. The leaves were separated into piles, or grades, starting at the top with small leaves called tips. Next came two grades of reds and then lugs. The bottom leaves could be separated into two grades of trash or lights, usually thin and light in weight and color and more ragged from growing close to the ground.

Anyone else who was available to help tied the grades into hands. Hands measured about two and a half inches at the top where the stems were placed, held evenly together, and squeezed to make a tight bundle. A carefully selected leaf folded and wrapped securely around the stem ends completed the hand. The finished hands were then put back onto the wooden sticks, into a tobacco press, and held there until all the tobacco was ready to be taken to market.

It was usually very cold at tobacco-stripping time. Workers wore layers of clothing to stay warm in barns that were not built to keep out the winter wind and cold. We usually had a fire going in a large metal drum or barrel or a woodburning stove that had been retired from the house. Sometimes Mom would throw potatoes and onions, skin on, into the ashes to bake. Pinto beans suspended over the fire and cooked for hours with a piece of fat pork tasted really good at the end of a long day in the cold barn.

MOUNTAIN MARTHA

Ed Burton used brown paper from a large roll to wrap goods when his customers bought something from his general store. Maxine saved the best of the paper and used it to make paper curtains, valances, and a mantel scarf. She carefully and skillfully scalloped the edges, cut heart shapes and star designs to create patterns in the paper, and then attached the pieces to cover the bare windows and to decorate the mantel. Her ability to improvise drew favorable comments from friends and family. In fact, one person remarked that she had successfully made an old shack look very much like a dollhouse.

The brown paper curtains were eventually replaced when Dad's older brother, Homer, and his wife, Hester, came for a visit bearing the wonderful gift of curtains made of serviceable fabric.

Their only household purchase was a bed, including mattress and springs, that they bought from Alma and Bud Reed's store, located near Elk Creek on Route 460. It cost a whopping twenty-five dollars. Bedding was borrowed from Lizzie.

Maxine had made several quilts before her marriage. However, she brought only one to her own household because they were needed and being used for the brothers and sisters she had left behind. Her mother, Lucy Belle Elam Crase, provided one teacup and two spoons from her own limited supply of household goods.

Eventually, Mom created sheets, pillowcases, and scarves sewed from feed sacks that were saved and given to her by her good friends, Ruth and Lola Reed.

THE INITIATION

A few days passed after the wedding, and Maxine started to miss her family. Ties were strong, and she had three brothers and three sisters still living at home. Because the distance was covered on foot or by horseback, a visit home would involve at least an overnight stay.

Camaraderie was good between Coy and her three brothers. At the start of their first visit home, the brothers set out for the barn to do chores with Coy, the new young husband, comfortably joining to help.

Later, Maxine saw him coming toward the house slinging his cap up and down and then from side to side. At some point, all the boys had stopped to relieve themselves behind the barn. In one swift motion, one of the brothers grabbed Coy's hat from his head and held it to Coy's front. Before he could physically do anything to stop it, the hat was full and very wet with his own pee. Coy had been initiated into the brotherhood in the typically creative Crase family fashion.

DON'T HIT HIM AGAIN!

Coy and Maxine settled into their little rented house and began their lives together on Settlement Branch. It didn't take long for neighbors to realize that they had a spitfire in their midst. Maxine was definitely not afraid to express her opinions or come to the aid of an oppressed individual.

Once when a neighbor was severely whipping his own nephew, Mom was walking by and yelled for him to stop. He didn't stop but yelled back, "Shut your mouth!" The man had been burning a broken handle out of an ax blade when he got angry at the boy for some unknown reason and began beating him. The man kept beating the boy, and Mom, in her anger and frustration, boldly walked to the site and kicked the ax, fire and all, into the creek. Whether she did it to distract the man or to release her own anger, I don't know, but her action worked to make him stop hitting the child. His attention turned toward dealing with the spunky character who had interrupted his day. Not knowing what else to do to handle this brazen young woman, the man got on his horse, rode to Long Branch, and brought her dad (Preacher Andy Crase) back to reprimand his daughter (my mom).

When Andy asked why she kicked the ax, she replied with a question: "Why was he beating that little boy?"

Grandpa Andy turned his horse and rode home without a word.

Mom was eight months pregnant with my sister, her first child, at the time.

Maxine Crase Patrick. She was a sassy girl!

*Maxine Crase Patrick. Still sassy! This picture was likely taken when
she was in her early seventies. She is now one hundred years old.*

TO GO OR TO STAY?

My sister Juanita was born on April 24, 1941. When she was five days old, Dad set out to find work in Cincinnati. Pressure from family members who had already relocated, along with a desire to have a better life, made the decision fairly easy. Coy got a job at Philip Carey and sent for Maxine and the new baby. City life was difficult for him, and after eleven months, he decided to quit his job and take his young family back to Kentucky.

He settled very comfortably, living in the house with his mam and pap, but Maxine was eager to begin life on their own. When she got nowhere trying to persuade him to make a move, she took things into her own hands and rented a place from Ev and Ora Rudd. Many years later, Mom and Dad would purchase this farm. It joins the Bud Reed–Jesse Williams farm, which they would buy in 1953.

Mom made her plans to move whether Coy was willing to go or not. He agreed to help her move their limited amount of household goods but declared he would not be staying. The house was on the main Johnson Fork Road and just under two miles from Mam and Pap. I recently learned that this is a common label in families who descend from Welsh, Scottish, and Irish roots.

All their belongings were loaded onto a small mule-drawn sled. As he helped her to unload, he began to change his mind about staying. He returned the mule and sled to his parents and walked back to their newly rented house, where they lived for about a year. When Ev and Ora came back from Cincinnati to claim the house, Mom and Dad moved to Turkey Branch, where I was born on June 5, 1944.

Mom is now one hundred years old, and she has a little trouble piecing together a timeline for moves between the first stay on Turkey Branch and Long Branch, which is the last place we lived before moving back to the cabin on Turkey Branch.

McCoy Patrick and baby Juanita on one of the very few occasions he ever wore a tie. Taken at the conservatory in Cincinnati.

WHAT MIGHT HAVE BEEN

At age ten, Mom (Maxine) went to live with her sister Eliza (Aunt Lizie) in Breathitt County, where the air was more conducive to her good health. She had been plagued with allergies and asthma for most of her young life.

Among the new friends she met there was a handsome boy named Denny. They were close to the same age and soon discovered they wanted to spend more time together outside of school and school activities. He began showing up each evening for short visits.

They enjoyed getting to know each other. He was well-mannered, didn't use bad language, and was always respectful of her and the adults in the household. Over the months and years, they spent many hours together. In the beginning, they were just two children playing, most often barefoot, as they grew together. A favorite quiet spot to talk was sitting on an old stone well box near the house.

As time passed, their friendship grew into something more special. Even though she cannot remember even a kiss or hand-holding, the affection was there, genuine and wholesome.

As they grew older, Sunday afternoons spent together became a regular event. They had the privilege of listening to music records on Aunt Lizie's Victrola. Denny favored two records, but Mom remembers only one. He loved the song "Lonesome Valley" and would play it over and over again. As I ponder the rest of this story, I wonder if this song held some significance in the way things turned out for him.

When Denny was old enough, he joined the CCC. The Civilian Conservation Corps (CCC) was a public work relief program that operated from 1933 to 1942 in the United States for unemployed, unmarried men from "relief families" as part of the New Deal. While he was away, she got a letter from him at least every other day, and she responded in kind.

On his return to Breathitt County, he discovered that his entire family was preparing to move to Winchester, Kentucky. He was expected to go, and relocation would be permanent. Today the distance would be a simple inconvenience, but to the young couple in those days, the distance was problematic.

When she didn't hear from him after the move, she assumed he had lost interest or found someone else. Many years later, she learned the real truth. He wrote to her often and gave the letters to his mother to be mailed. His mother was concerned that he would eventually marry and move back to Breathitt County. She felt strongly about keeping her family close to her. For that reason, she did not post the letters.

Finally, Denny established communication through written letters to Aunt Lizie. Lizie wrote back telling Denny that Mom had met and made a promise to marry Coy. He quickly wrote again, asking Maxine not to proceed until he came to talk to her. Mom's reply: it's too late!

Denny eventually married and had a family.

In September 1955, Denny's life ended suddenly and tragically.

Aunt Lizie was the first to hear about his death. Guessing the impact the news would have on Mom, she and Uncle Chester drove to Magoffin County to be with Mom when she learned of the tragedy.

Mom and Dad had been married for several years. My sister was fourteen years old, and I was eleven at the time.

Mom was saddened at the news and grieved for the loss. She asked Dad to give her time and space to deal with her feelings. Dad was kind and understanding, and he supported her wishes.

Many years later, Mom heard from Denny's younger sister, who was able to fill in some gaps in the story.

Denny's mother regretted withholding the letters and was haunted by the question of what might have been had she not interfered.

BURLAP SACK—A GOOD SIGN

Depending on the seasons and work available, Dad did daywork for local farmers and landowners. He might be paid as little as two dollars or as much as eight for a long day of labor. There was no such thing as an eight-hour workday. He was expected to work from sunup to sundown.

If in the morning Dad left home carrying an empty burlap sack, we could expect one of two things upon his return.

From the mouth of Long Branch to our home, several small exposed veins of coal stuck out along the old and well-worn path that hugged the hillsides and avoided cutting through precious and profitable bottomland. Sometimes in the winter, he would stop to pick and gather coal for our fireplace. A sack full of coal would keep us warm for two or three days.

If it was very cold, ice would form on the cliffs and near the creek bed, and Dad would fill the burlap sack with ice. Cream from our own milk cow and eggs from our chickens were combined with a little sugar and vanilla from Ed Burton's store. A small pan with ears (handles), filled with the ingredients and covered well, was put into a larger pan. The space between the pans was filled with salt and the ice Dad had collected. While we waited, Mom or Dad would turn the small pan back and forth until we had ice cream! For us, at that time, ice cream was a wintertime treat.

THE HORSE TRADER

Dad was hardworking, but Mom was better with business and home management. Dad was a shrewd trader who learned valuable lessons through making some mistakes.

I never heard the words "career" or "career opportunity" in those days. A person earned a living doing whatever work they were strong enough to handle or whatever they could come up with to trade or barter. Dad worked for other farmers doing manual labor, but he most loved to negotiate simple deals involving livestock, farm tools, etc. Most everything was fair game. A person who made that a means of earning income was often labeled "horse trader."

It is said that when my sister, Juanita, was very young and just able to talk, if someone asked, "What does your daddy do?" she would reply, "He is a horse turder." Her way of saying horse trader.

Dad once traded Mom's eyeglasses for four bushels of corn and a goose.

On another occasion, he bought a sow and pigs, only to discover that the smallest piglet was nicely rounded because it had been born without the orifice for eliminating waste.

Friend and neighbor Charlie Purcell was the local expert on pig castration. Pigs fatten better into hogs when this procedure is done. Charlie and Dad prepared to relieve the unfortunate little pig and surgically create the orifice that nature had not provided for it. With the first incision, the pressure was very rapidly released, and the resulting spew covered the surgical team (Dad and Charlie) from head to toe.

To this day I remember with fondness the sweat-soaked smell of my dad's red plaid corduroy cap. I loved him dearly. He died too soon at fifty-one.

NORMA PATRICK SETO

SANTA FROM A WALNUT TREE

We were dependent on the growing cycles of crops, as well as wild growing things. Each season brought certain opportunities for adding to the family resources.

Walnut trees grew well on Long Branch, and the fall would find us gathering walnuts. The outside hulls were removed, and the nuts were spread to dry, or season, in their shells. I have memories of sitting around the fire, taking turns with the hammers and flat irons needed to free the nut meat from the hard shells. A flat iron turned upside down and held between the knees was the perfect surface for cracking the walnuts. It was important to hit hard enough to crack the shell but not hard enough to shatter the nut meat inside. There were contests to see who could shell out the biggest piece of nut kernel.

The nut meats were carefully separated and spread on feed sacks to dry. Packing too soon would result in mold, especially if the walnuts were less than well-seasoned. We saved a small amount for our own use, but most were shipped for a cash return. Each season brought a different and unique way to make money, and every bit helped.

The last year we lived on Long Branch, Mom shipped twenty-two pounds of walnuts at nineteen cents a pound, yielding $4.18. With that money, she bought a small red rocking chair, two dolls, and a tea set for my sister and me for Christmas.

Because I don't want to forget the old ways, I will seek out a productive tree in the fall and collect a few walnuts. Cracking the shells and removing the nut kernels is a slow and tedious process.

Recently I sat using a hammer to crack the walnuts I had saved from a previous year. It took a long time to yield just one cup full. I thought about how difficult it must have been and how many hours it took for Mom to get twenty-two pounds to ship and sell. Once my cup was full, I went inside and thanked her for the rocking chair, tea set, and dolls that she worked hard so many years ago to get for my sister and me.

Juanita Patrick Richter, circa 1943.

I SAW IT WITH MY OWN EYES!

I t was Christmas Eve. The kerosene lamps had been snuffed out. Fire from the fireplace burned brightly, and the four of us were huddled close for the warmth of it. All of a sudden, Dad put his hands into the fireplace and just above the flames in time to catch a whole box of Mounds candy bars. Santa was right on time. He had not forgotten two little girls and their parents in the hills of eastern Kentucky. And that Santa! He knew Mom liked Mounds candy bars!

That is exactly how I remember the episode, but my adult mind wants to interfere with a beautiful childhood experience and tell you that Dad probably drew our attention away with an "oh look" and a pointing finger. He must have tossed the candy "up" the chimney while we were distracted, only to catch it when we looked back. And with perfect timing. I like my child memory much better.

Christmas trees were selected and cut from the nearby hillside or field, carried home, and decorated with pieces of cotton, strings of popcorn, colorful crepe paper left over from Decoration Day flower making, foil scraps saved from gum wrappers, and ornaments made from natural things like balls from sycamore trees.

CHRISTMAS PACKAGES

Brown paper packages tied up with string sometimes arrived at the post office for us at Christmas.

The Epson, Kentucky, post office served the families on Johnson Fork, including Long Branch, Tim Branch, and other tributaries and hollers off the main road. It took up only a small space in the corner of Ed Burton's store. Each day the mail would arrive by mule, and Ed or his wife, Gleedie, would "shift" the mail, taking out what was addressed to local folks and sending the rest to the next community up the road. The mail carrier also took with him any outgoing mail.

There was a little post office at least every two to five miles. Elsie, Kentucky, was close to the mouth of Johnson Fork on Highway 460. There might have been one in between. Then there was Stella on Cow Creek Run by Mary and Lonnie Dunn, and Kernie at the mouth of Cow Creek by Garland and Mary Louise Dunn. On Johnson Fork there was Hager, Kentucky, at the mouth of Turkey Branch, operated by Vivian Purcell. At the mouth of Long Branch was Epson, Kentucky, which was run by Ed and Gleedie Burton out of their general store. Farther on was Nettie, Kentucky, run by Buford and Myrtle Patrick. Burg, Kentucky, was on Wheelrim, which branches off Johnson Fork.

The general store and post office in Epson, Kentucky, circa 1940, with proprietors Ed and Gleedie Burton seated on the porch. When Tim Branch School burned, it carried on temporarily at this location. I remember well what the inside of this building was like. It was filled with groceries, animal feed, and other dry goods. It is hard to imagine how classes were carried out, but the Burtons were very gracious to share the space.

A LOVELY STORY

Mom and Dad were both from large families. Some of their brothers and sisters left eastern Kentucky to find work. Most of them prospered and returned for periodic visits, which we thoroughly enjoyed. Almost all of the relatives who left Magoffin County kept in touch by sending cards and letters.

Uncle Freeling Patrick, his wife, Verlene, and their daughters, Carol and Anita, often remembered us with Christmas packages of fruit, candy, toys, and clothes.

Aunt Becky, Dad's sister, left Settlement Branch to find a job in Cincinnati. Coincidentally, a young man named Harkes Johnson, who lived just around the hillside on another fork of Settlement Branch, left at about the same time and for the same purpose. They arrived separately in the big city. Each found employment, and at some point, they met and fell in love. They got married and had three lovely daughters.

As her own family grew, Aunt Becky remembered us, especially at Christmastime. We looked forward to the boxes she sent.

When my sister and I made our own decisions to relocate and move to Cincinnati, Aunt Becky and Uncle Hark were there to help make the transition easier. Aunt Becky never turned away a relative who needed lodging, and she freely gave her own unique style of encouragement. There are things about me that I attribute to the strong influence of Aunt Becky. She encouraged a high personal standard and was not timid about voicing her opinion regarding life choices that I (and others) made.

In a recent conversation I had with Leah, we got around to

talking about toys, more specifically about dolls we had when we were little. When I asked if she kept her dolls, she replied, "No. I think we sent them all to you." It's true! They sent not only toys and dolls but clothing as well.

The following poem, which I wrote as a tribute to Becky's daughter Iva, also reflects on the parents who raised her and the sisters she grew up with.

Iva …
Iva story to tell
Iva song to sing
Iva flag to wave
Iva bell to ring
—about Iva
Iva gift to give
Iva prayer to pray
Iva life to live
Iva game to play
—that's Iva
Iva coin to spend
Iva place to sleep
Iva coat to wear
Iva meal to eat
—from Iva
Iva many friends
Iva life of giving
Iva smile for all
Iva love for living
—oh Iva!

—Norma Seto, 1990

POKE GREENS

I love poke greens, poke weed, poke salad. It is the same plant called by different names. I've decided that if you didn't grow up eating and appreciating poke, you will likely never understand or develop a taste for it. To most folks, it is just a weed. To others, it is a delicacy! Luckily for me, it grows almost everywhere, and no matter where I happen to be in the spring, I will find some to cook and enjoy, even if it means invading someone's backyard. My son, Matthew, fights the battle of the poke weed in his yard, but he is usually very good to save some for me.

Mom always cooked the leaves and then fried them in a little bacon fat. The stalks were cut into rounds, dipped in egg, rolled in cornmeal with a little salt and pepper, and then fried until golden and crisp.

I usually fix the leaves and stalks separately (as described above) and serve them combined in the same dish.

MOUNTAIN TEA

Another wild treat could be found as we traveled the paths through the woods leading to Grandma's or to the general store. Mountain tea is a small plant that has a white blossom on it in the spring and early summer. The green leaves have a shiny surface. The fruit is a very small pea-sized red berry that is safe to eat. We chewed the leaves for the flavor only and then spit them out. I still like a nice chew of the plant, which tastes very much like Teaberry chewing gum, and I am always on the lookout for it as I enjoy one of my very favorite pastimes: walking in the woods.

BANTY HEN AND A BUFFALO BAG

Mom once set a banty hen on regular-sized hen eggs and set another banty hen on banty eggs. After three weeks, all the eggs hatched—small banty chicks from one hen and regular-sized chicks from the other. For some unknown reason, Mom decided to "break" one hen and combine the chicks to be raised by the other hen. It didn't take long to realize that the selected hen was not going to accept the larger chicks. She viciously pecked at the big chicks until she killed three of them. Because the second hen had been "broken up," she had no interest in taking back her hatchlings.

Mom put the frustrated hen with all the chicks into a large paper box and took them inside the house, where she could keep an eye on them while she tried to come up with a solution.

Mom was persistent! She decided that if the hen could not *see* the large chicks, she would not be able to distinguish the differences in the brood.

In those days, most of the men in the family were smokers. There were two brands of loose tobacco available at the general store. The preferred brand was Prince Albert in a can, and the second was Buffalo tobacco, which was packaged in a small muslin bag with a yellow drawstring closure. An empty Buffalo tobacco bag was the perfect size to fit over the hen's head. Mom tied the tobacco sack securely over the head of the hen and put her back inside the box with the baby chicks, big and small. She could not eat or drink and would run into the sides of the box. At intervals, Mom would remove the bag and set the hen outside the box so she could have food and water.

Mom kept trying to get the hen to accept all the chicks.

Good friend and neighbor Mary Louise Dunn found all this very entertaining. She would come for a visit just to watch the angry and frustrated hen bounce off the sides of the box.

Finally, Mom had to give up on the hen. She threw her out of the box and hand-raised all the chicks without the benefit of a mama hen.

MEMORIES OF UNCLE VENCIN

Uncle Vencin, Dad's brother, was almost always nearby. He never married, and he lived with Grandma and Grandpa until they died. In fact, it appeared that he was singled out and groomed to be the one to take care of them through their old age.

He directed much of his affection and attention to my sister and me. He was like a third parent who did only fun things with us. He didn't have to get involved with discipline, and any lessons learned from him were painless and enjoyable.

On one occasion, Mom and Dad were called away to help with someone who was sick. Because they couldn't be sure how long they would be needed, they asked Vencin to stay with Juanita and me.

It was understood by all that the job involved much more than just taking care of us. The pig, chickens, and cow were to be fed; there were eggs to be gathered; and above all, the cow had to be milked.

We always had at least one milk cow. In fact, in the early years I don't ever remember being without a cow, but neither do I remember having more than one.

Vencin delighted in making us happy. Whether we suggested he get the cow on the back porch to milk her or it was strictly his idea, I do not recall. What stays vividly in my mind were the peals of laughter at seeing the cow on the porch. Vencin squirted most of the milk into the bucket, but some of the warm white streams went flying to the mouths of the cats and kittens, who caught on very quickly, to their good fortune. Of course, he directed some toward our feet to make us dance and jump as we squealed with glee.

We were heard at least a half mile down the road by our parents ... who came home a little before they were expected.

Norma Patrick Seto

Maxine Patrick, McCoy Patrick, and Vencin Patrick, circa 1940.

A VERY FAT LIP

Occasionally in the spring, Dad and Vencin would go into the woods in search of bee trees. Bees find a hollow tree and move their swarm into the cavity, where they can live and produce their honey undisturbed. Bees are wild by nature, and they like to locate their hives in the woods, in a tree, a fair height off the ground.

When a bee tree was spotted and marked, Dad and Vencin would return later, equipped with whatever was needed to cut and remove the two to three-foot section occupied by the bees. The cutting and retrieving was usually done just past dusk, when the hive was quiet for the night. Leaving the bees in the cut section created a natural hive that could be sealed off until it was moved to a spot near the house. A smooth, flat rock functioned as the base for the hive. A wide board covered the top and was weighted down by a heavy rock.

The hive was given a few weeks to get established and manufacture enough honey for themselves and our family. When it was time, the honey was taken from the hive and enjoyed on our table at every meal. We called that robbing the bees.

The bee equipment was not sophisticated. A twisted burning rag sufficed until Uncle Vencin came by a smoker. Headgear was simply screen wire or thin see-through cloth draped over a wide-brimmed hat, wrapped, and shaped around the face to protect the "robber" from stings.

Late one Saturday evening, it was decided that it was time to rob the beehives. I kept a safe distance as I watched Uncle Vencin slowly remove the board from atop a hive. With a large knife, he carefully cut chunks of honey from the primitive hive and placed them in an aluminum dishpan. As the honey accumulated in the pan, it started to look very tempting. I became braver and stepped forward. Honey is warm and delicious when it is first removed from the hive. I quickly and stealthily grabbed a chunk of honeycomb. I took a bite without examining the piece. I did not see the bee that was still clinging to the product of his hard work. I knew the second I put it to my mouth that my lower lip got the full impact of his stinger. It started to hurt and swell immediately. The lip ended up being about three times its normal size. It felt so tight I thought it might split.

The next day was Sunday, and this girl went to church with a very fat lip!

The lesson: it is safer to rob the hive than it is to steal from the pan.

HOW HIGH CAN YOU KICK, EARL?

When the day was done and darkness came, Mom sewed to make quilts. Sewing by the light of coal oil (kerosene) lamps was difficult, but she produced many beautiful quilts in creative patterns, all stitched and quilted by hand. The fabric she used was taken from clothing scraps, feed sacking, or pieces that were given or traded from other women.

When all the pieces were put together to form the quilt top, she would then tack it into the frames with a lining and batting. The frames were suspended from the ceiling, and when she wasn't actively quilting, the frame and quilt could be rolled up to the ceiling to get it out of the way.

It was fun and cozy to play under the quilt as she stitched. A sharp rap on the head with the thimbled finger told us when we were getting too rowdy.

Mom usually kept a few pieces of hard candy on the quilt top for her own enjoyment as she worked. If our behavior was good as we played under the framed quilt, we could expect a piece to be shared.

Earl Walters, a friend of Dad's, would stop by periodically to visit, share tall tales, and gossip. He was a tall, long-legged man, and in winter he wore gum boots that came almost to his knees.

One day as he warmed his backside by our fire, he wondered if he could kick high enough to kick the rolled-up quilt out of the frame. Things to do for entertainment were very limited. As Earl pondered the possibility, Dad became intrigued, and though he didn't encourage Earl, he didn't make any effort to stop him. The satisfaction of successfully kicking the quilt out of the frame was short-lived and not worth the wrath that came down upon them from the quilter.

QUILTS AND KITTENS PREDICT NUPTIALS

I try to get with old school friends when I go back to eastern Kentucky. Several of us gather around 8:30 a.m. at McDonalds in Salyersville. We have a cup of coffee and a little breakfast and enjoy each other's company until the lunch crowd starts to push us out around noon.

Many of our stories are repeated each time we get together. They never get old to us. The shared memories and the laughter that ensues keeps us connected and happy to be together.

Occasionally, a story or memory will surface that is new to me. One of my friends told this story at our last get-together.

She asked how my ninety-seven-year-old mom was doing. Mom is the only surviving parent among my friends in this group. I reported that Mom was doing well and that she was still working on quilt squares. Women in that area and era made quilts not only as a hobby but for the practical purpose of keeping the family protected against the cold winters. My friend's mother was no exception.

The conversation eventually went to the art of quilt making, traditions, and superstitions connected with the activity.

My friend said that when her mother finished a quilt, she would instruct someone to "go get the cat." Once the cat was brought inside, all the single people in the family and neighborhood would find a spot around the quilt. The cat was placed in the center and the single people surrounding the quilt would grab on and shake the quilt until the cat became scared or agitated and ran off the quilt. The person the cat ran off closest to was said to be the one who would be next to marry.

Now, at some point I started to wonder why I had never heard of this tradition. When I asked Mom if she knew about it, she explained that her family for years did the same thing, but then she explained why it was stopped.

With the help of her daughters, Grandma had finished a beautiful quilt, positioned every unmarried person around it, and instructed one of my aunts to "go get the cat." She came back with a sickly kitten. When the kitten was placed in the center of the beautiful quilt, it scurried around the quilt for much longer than expected. As it ran frantically all around the quilt, it squirted on many spots, nearly ruining it.

At that point, the "cat on the quilt" method of predicting the next wedding was abandoned by the Crase family.

A DARK AND SCARY NIGHT

The typical noises heard at night were the natural sounds of crickets and whippoorwills. As a rule, neighbors and family members did not come around after dark unless something was seriously wrong.

I remember on one occasion when the peaceful sounds were interrupted by the sound of horses' hooves, faintly at first and then louder as we realized they were coming to our house. Concerned looks passed between Mom and Dad as they recognized Mom's brother and that he was drunk. He was not a pleasant fellow when he was drinking, and what's more, he had several friends riding with him who were very unpredictable and drunk as well. There were tense moments as Dad went outside and told them to ride on. Peeking through the window, I could see the dark shadows of the horses and riders and hear the snorting and stomping of the horses' feet as the riders considered for a few moments and then rode away without an argument.

CANDY PARTY

Social events usually centered around church and family activities. One exception stands out.

A group of teens and young adults would get together and decide to come to our house for a "candy party." Mom had a reputation for making excellent fudge, chocolate or vanilla.

We seldom had a shortage of butter and milk, but if a large amount of fudge was expected, the friends knew to bring sugar and cocoa. Though it might be discovered later that they had stopped at Burton's store, made the purchase, and charged it to my dad's account. Twenty-five cents was once charged to our account when one of the partygoers had been thoughtful to bring coal oil, which was needed to keep the lamps burning.

The group never announced plans; they simply showed up with the necessary ingredients and a big appetite for fudge.

The party centered on the making of the fudge, and Mom would get right to the task as the friends told stories and played games. Friends always arrived before dark, but the fun would last well into the evening, and some of the group would occasionally stay overnight.

Getting to scrape the pot was my favorite part; I was always warned not to scrape too hard for fear I'd scrape the glaze off the pan and it would make me sick.

Bennett and Pauline Arnett lived more than a half mile down the holler and out on the main road. It was said that when Pauline's brother was visiting, he would step out onto their porch and sniff the air for cooking fudge. When his sensitive nose picked up the smell coming from our kitchen, he would come running to join the "candy party."

I LEARN TO CUSS!

One fine summer day, Mom and her good friend Gleedie Burton decided to go blackberry picking. Juanita and Gleedie's daughters, Opal and Gaye, were old enough to go along, and they were the perfect age to learn from their mothers about gathering berries and enjoying friendship while working together.

I was not quite old enough to keep up as they scoured the hills and hollows in search of berries. It was my good fortune to stay with Ed Burton, the storekeeper-postmaster. Ed liked to talk. He had strong opinions about most things, and his conversation was enhanced liberally with swear words. There was very little dialogue between the two of us on that day, but I listened very closely to the talk between Ed and the people who came to the store and the post office.

Several days later, I was having trouble getting our screen door to close. The house on Long Branch was very old and in poor condition when we moved into it. Except for very minor repairs, no effort was made to improve it as long as we lived there. In my frustration, I let loose with a few words that got my mom's attention. I was probably between three and four years old.

When the screen door got the benefit of my expanded vocabulary, my shocked mom asked how I knew such words. I proudly told her that I had learned them from Ed Burton. Funny, I don't remember ever being left to stay with Ed after that day.

My daughter Bethany asked if I remember specifically what the cuss words were. Yes, I remember, but it would not be appropriate to list them here.

*McCoy Patrick. Taken in front of our home on Long Branch. Normalene is
standing in the background on the porch near the above-mentioned screen door.*

CHOCOLATE GRAVY

1/4 cup flour
1 cup sugar
3 tablespoons cocoa powder
2 cups milk
1 teaspoon vanilla
Butter to taste

Combine ingredients. Bring to boil over medium high heat. Stir until thickened. Serve over homemade biscuits.

Some memories are like a photograph and are often brought to mind by a familiar smell. Melting butter dropped into a pan of steaming chocolate gravy and served over fluffy hot biscuits was a favorite breakfast enjoyed in the cabin on Turkey Branch.

The cast-iron woodburning stove sat in the corner of the lean-to kitchen. The floor sagged under the weight of it. Warmth in the room was much more than the heat generated by the hot fire in the stove. I remember Dad gently chiding, sometimes stroking my mom. The feelings of belonging, being loved, and feeling safe were far more important than any material things that we lacked.

One of two "winderlights" (windows) looked out upon the end of the little valley. Several hills came together to form the ridge encircling the knoll upon which the cabin rested. A short walk down the knoll brought us to the spring, which provided cool mountain water and served to keep butter and milk cold.

From the spring and straight up the hillside, we could take the familiar path that led through the woods and down to Ed Burton's store.

The basic cabin was strong and solidly built. The first level was one simple room with an open fireplace. There was one small "winderlight" at the front of the room, directly opposite the opening to the kitchen. The front door led outside to a porch, about six feet deep and eight feet long. The step leading into the yard was simply a well-shaped field stone.

The yard was flat, free of grass, and kept free of twigs and debris by Mom, who regularly swept the yard. A visitor's impression of a homemaker's habits and skills was often formed at the edge of the yard and well before walking through the front door.

A well-swept yard was also necessary for successful marble games. The Keeton family lived around the hillside from the cabin. Teenagers Robert, Ralph, and Rodney were the youngest of the large family and were still living at home. Twenty-something-year-old Dad still enjoyed playing games and spending time with the boys. They would arrive with their own collection of marbles saved in a poke or a can. A circle was drawn in the nicely swept yard. The players would get down on hands and knees, and a serious game of marbles would begin, sometimes lasting until dark.

In winter when marble games were no longer practical, Ralph, Rodney, and Robert would show up with their homemade checkerboard. The checker pieces made a distinct sound as they bounced against the sides of the can. The sound would vary depending on how fast the boys were walking or running, eager to involve Dad in a serious game of checkers. I recently asked if the old checkerboard is still around. It is! Safely kept and cherished by a member of another generation of the Keeton family.

BORN COOPERATIVE

We lived in the Turkey Branch cabin when I was born in June 1944, moved to and lived at several other places, and then moved back to the cabin on Turkey Branch when I was five.

On June 4, 1944, Mom went to fetch water from the spring, and when she bent to scoop up the water, her garment split right up the back. Mom called the dress her "Hoover apron," which she defines as a wraparound maternity dress. I was a ten-pound, two-ounce baby, and I was pushing the threads and fabric to the limit.

She walked back up the hill to the cabin and declared to my dad, "If this baby is not born tomorrow, I don't have a thing to wear." Being always cooperative, I made my appearance the following day. She saved the scraps and fabric from the dress, and over the following weeks, she incorporated the pieces into a quilt, which is now displayed proudly on the wall behind her bed at my place. I love looking at the quilt, showing it, and telling the story.

Mom was assisted in the delivery by Dr. Barnes Conley, who was driven by motorized vehicle to the mouth of Johnson Fork. From there he rode a horse to the cabin on Turkey Branch. At that time, Monroe Davis and his family lived in a house just at the point where the path turns up the hill to go to the cabin. A day or so after I was born, Monroe's young son, J.M., made his way up to the cabin and asked to see the new baby. When Mom asked how he knew she had a baby, J.M., who was probably four years old at the time, said he saw my head sticking out of the saddlebag as the doctor rode by on his way to "deliver" me.

I was born in this cabin on June 5, 1944. We moved from here to the Jesse Williams place and then to Long Branch. The family moved back here when I was five or six. In this picture, the chimney has fallen away (left side of the photo) The basic cabin was still very solid.

The cabin as it is now. Renovated and now equipped with indoor plumbing and electricity. John D. Holbrook and Maxine Crase Patrick are sitting on the porch.

Norma Patrick Seto

FLU RESISTANT

I have a vague memory of sitting behind the stove long after fire had gone out, leaving the house very cold.

Mom, Dad, and Juanita all had a serious case of the flu and were unable to care for the healthy one, who was too young to care for herself. Me! I was between two and three years old.

One evening after dark, Mom's brother Kiser just happened to come by for a visit. He recognized the problem and began hurriedly to take care of the most urgent need. He grabbed an ax and pried a board from the end of the porch. He split the wood and used the pieces to build a fire. He then went to fetch more help.

One of my twin aunts came to the rescue. When she arrived, my then sixteen-year-old aunt quickly restoked the fire and began cooking food. She also took on the task of caring for the sick.

I was told that I was very emotional and glad to see all that my aunt was doing. I cried as I sat in the warm room, eating the good meal she had prepared. Mom estimates I had not eaten and had been ignored for at least two days.

Thank you, dear aunt!

RAIN ON THE METAL ROOF

Steep, narrow stairs led up to the second level of the cabin on Turkey Branch. The space under the stairs provided the only "closet" space and was used to store "canned stuff" of meats, fruits, and vegetables as well as potatoes, pumpkins, shoes, and clothing.

The second level of the cabin was much like the first, including a door that led out onto a second-level porch. We were never permitted to go out onto the second-level porch because even at that time the porch had started to give way at one end.

The upstairs had two "winderlights."

From the second level of the cabin, we could hear the wonderful sound of rain hitting the tin roof, and on rainy days, my sister and I played paper dolls, cut from the pages of a Sears Roebuck Catalog. Our cousin Myrtle showed us how to glue catalog pages to cardboard and, once the glue was dry, cut carefully around any item we liked. A simple slit here and there allowed us to wear fine paper watches and jewelry. The possibilities were endless; we were deprived of nothing within the pages of the Sears Roebuck Catalog. Furniture, luggage, pots, pans, dishes—all was available to us and made of paper, glue, and cardboard.

I credit my cousin Myrtle, whose creativity inspired me early and led to a lifelong interest and work in graphic art and design.

THE ROCK AND THE ROOSTER

My sister and I walked from the head of Turkey Branch out to the main road and another quarter mile to school. We were usually late. Distance was a factor, but we also had to cross a small stream (branch) a few times as we followed the path out to the main road. Very often one of us would accidentally fall into water and have to go home for dry clothes.

Twice a day, going to and from school, I walked by the "rock that's as big as a house," hoping a rooster would crow. The big rock is near a barn, which was home to several hens and a rooster.

A path snaked behind the rock and the barn. It led up the holler and over the hills to Grandma and Grandpa's house and to Uncle Vencin, who lived with them. We considered ourselves very fortunate on the occasions Uncle Vencin walked the path with us. Without fail, every time we passed by the "rock that's as big as a house," Uncle Vencin would say, "That rock turns over every time it hears a rooster crow."

Whatever Uncle Vencin said was believable. In my mind, he was totally credible and to be trusted without question. So it was just a matter of time, patience, and good planning to be there at the moment when that rooster did his miraculous deed.

The "rock that's as big as a house" never did turn over, despite its close proximity to the barn and its resident rooster.

I don't remember if enlightenment came through my parents or if one day it occurred through insight that the "rock that's as big as a house" doesn't have ears! It can't hear a rooster crow.

The confidence that Uncle Vencin would never lie to me was not shaken, but I did learn to listen a little more carefully when someone made a claim that touched on the realm of impossibility.

Turkey Branch School. Sometime in the early 1960s, I took pictures of the school and its surroundings. There is now a house where the school once stood.

TURKEY BRANCH SCHOOL

Turkey Branch School was a one-room schoolhouse. Several high windows were installed along the side of the building facing the road. Shelves along the wall under the windows held books to accommodate students, grades one through eight, in all subjects. A cloakroom along the front was accessible through a door immediately to the right of the schoolhouse main entrance. The cloakroom exited at the opposite side, where a triangular corner shelf held a water bucket and dipper. Older students kept the water bucket filled by going to the well house, which was located at the edge of the schoolyard.

At the beginning of the school year, each student was asked to bring a drinking cup from home for individual use. Each cup varied in color, material, and size, so there was little need to mark them for identification. Each person recognized his or her own cup.

All grades enjoyed a morning and afternoon recess. When the weather permitted outdoor activity, we played Annie, Annie Over, tag, base, drop the hanky, farmer in the dell, red rover, and crack the whip.

Annie, Annie Over is played over a building that is low enough for a ball to be thrown over it. The area of the building must be small enough that players can run all the way around it. Team one calls out, "Annie, Annie Over," and throws the ball over the building to the players on team two. If the ball is not caught by team two, that team can wait a moment (to keep team one guessing if it was caught or missed), yell "Annie, Annie Over," and throw the ball back. If team two catches the ball, they try to sneak around the building to tag a member or members of team one. If a player is tagged, that person becomes part of the opposing team. The game starts with an even number of people on each side. If the ball doesn't go over the building when thrown, the thrower yells, "Pigtail!", and tries to throw it again. The losing team is determined when the last player on that team is tagged.

In drop the hankie, children form a circle and stand (or sit) facing each other. One child is chosen to be "it" by drawing straws or guessing a number. The child who is "it" holds a handkerchief and begins running around the outside of the circle. He or she eventually drops the hanky behind one of the other children and takes off running as fast as he or she can. The child behind whom the hanky was dropped picks it up and runs after and tries to catch the "it" child. The "it" child's goal is to run completely around the circle and get back to the open space before the child with the hanky tags him or her.

If the child with the hanky catches the "it" child, the "it" child must be "it" again and try once more to get a spot in the circle. If the child holding the hanky does not catch "it" before "it" gets back to the spot, then the child holding the hanky becomes "it" and the process starts all over again.

Bluebird, bluebird is based around the song:

> Bluebird, bluebird, in and out my window.
> Bluebird, bluebird, in and out my window.
> Bluebird, bluebird, in and out my window.
> Oh, Johnny, I'm tired.
> Take a little girl and tap her on the shoulder.
> Take a little girl and tap her on the shoulder.
> Take a little girl and tap her on the shoulder.
> Oh, Johnny, I'm tired.

The children stand in a circle, holding hands high up in arches (to form the "windows" in the song). One child is the blue bird who flies in and out of the arches or "windows." During the second verse, the "bird" chooses a partner by patting him or her on the shoulder. The second child then follows, holding the first child's shoulders while they pass through the "windows." The game continues until all the children make a chain and there are only two children left forming an arch. They then become the first two bluebirds in the next round.

A favorite recess activity of the boys was to sit on the hillside and throw small stones onto the metal roof of the girls toilet.

In summertime, the girls made a playhouse under a large hickory tree behind the school and slightly up the hillside. Rocks, twigs, tin cans, etc. were used to create furnishings for the pretend home. When weather was nice, we carried our lunch pails up to the hickory tree and ate there. Some girls had regular store-bought lunch pails, but most brought food in a four-pound lard bucket.

Margie Lykins was my first-grade teacher. I remember only that she was young and pretty. She had long curly dark red hair.

A blackboard covered most of the back wall. The door to the coal room was at the left on the back wall. Coal fueled the potbellied stove, which was our source of heat in winter. One of the older boys was paid ten cents a week to get to school and build a fire in the stove before the teacher and other students arrived.

It took some time in winter for the potbellied stove to warm the large, high-ceilinged single room that served the entire student population of Turkey Branch School.

Seats were of the same style for all grades. The desks for grades one through five accommodated one small person. Each seat was designed so that the desk of one person provided a seat for the person in front. Desks for grades six through eight were the same design but wider to hold two students and sometimes three.

On very cold mornings, we would pull the seats close to the stove, which sometimes glowed red hot.

On one such morning, I was sitting on a wide-style seat pulled within two feet of the hot stove. Two younger students shared the seat, and the three of us had taken our shoes off and tucked our feet under us for comfort and added warmth. A heavy boy was sitting on the desk part of the unit. He was distracted by something and jumped up. The balance of weight shifted, and the seat started to fall forward. With my feet tucked under me, there was no other choice but to put my hands on the hot rim of the cast-iron stove to stop the three of us from falling face-first onto the hot metal. I was oldest of the three and had (still do) exceptionally long arms for my height and build. Though I kept no scars on my hands, my mind will carry the imprint of that moment forever.

Another blackboard ran along the side wall opposite the windows. The back door to the schoolhouse was to the left on the side wall as well. In warm weather, the doors remained open. Grades were separated by rows, starting with first grade on the right as we entered. I remember looking out the open back door on my first day of school. Tall yellow grass swayed in the late August heat, and I sat in the first-grade row, wishing I could be at home.

Seats faced away from the entrance, toward the blackboard and the coal room door. As the rows got near the windows, the grades got higher, ending with eighth grade right under the window and near the bookshelves.

The stove was located in front of the seventh and eighth grade rows. Safer maybe, but that also meant the smaller children were farther away from heat in winter.

When the teacher rang the school bell, she also called out, "Books!" The word had a different connotation for us and meant the beginning of school or classes. The words "take up books" had the same meaning as "ring the school bell for classes to begin."

There was no need to ask permission to go to the toilet. A small cardboard with a loop of string hung over a nail at the entrance to the room. The word "IN" was hand-lettered on one side and "OUT" on the opposite side. When the word "IN" was visible, it meant everyone was inside and you simply turned the board on the way out to show that someone had gone out. It was equally important to others to remember to flip the card again upon your return, thus giving another student the signal that it was okay to go out.

A narrow path led to the boys toilet and continued to the girls toilet a few yards on. The toilets were simple unpainted wooden one-holers. No water or means of hand washing was available. What's more, no toilet paper was provided… ever! One provided for oneself by having paper in a pocket in advance of the need. Most of the girls had a hiding place in the toilet. Small pieces of notebook paper, catalog tear outs, or tissue would be stuck under a board, behind the support post, or between the roof and rafters of the toilet. What a crisis to discover, just at the point of greatest need, that someone had found your hiding place and used your paper.

The boys toilet was in front on the path. The
girls toilet was a few yards beyond.

Discipline was determined by the one teacher who was employed to instruct all the children attending the one-room school. Some were effective in getting top performance from the children with a minimal amount of physical punishment. Other teachers resorted to the hickory switch at any minor infraction. The switches were cut daily from the large hickory tree that grew just behind the schoolhouse. There was no monitoring or direction given from a higher authority in the school system as to how severe the whippings should or could be, and school officials never followed up for any incident. Discipline was left completely to the discretion of the person in charge. Only once did I witness punishment that was too severe and unfair, but it was enough to impress my memory for almost seventy years.

To stand with your "nose in the ring" was a common form of punishment; it was uncomfortable and humiliating but not necessarily painful. I experienced it once because I was talking at the blackboard when I should have been working. I was asked to step close enough to the blackboard that my nose touched and then instructed to pull up on tiptoe. A ring was then drawn on the board and the offending student (in this case me) was told to keep his or her nose in the drawn ring while standing on tiptoe for the amount of time determined by the teacher.

MISSIONARIES AND FLANNEL GRAPH

The missionaries came to school once a week to give a lesson and to tell Bible stories. We looked forward to the flannel graph picture display and the soothing, though different, voices of the women who had come into eastern Kentucky to teach boys and girls about Jesus. I never knew their history, where they came from, or their church affiliation. But they came with a real commitment to the task. The two I remember were there for most of their adult lives. Miss Lamb had been around for a few years before I started first grade. She lived in a small cabin that had been built for her on a section of property donated by local farmer Bruner Arnett. She rode a horse for transportation. In fact, Mom remembers that Miss Lamb would sometimes spend nights with us to share and enjoy food and shelter. Dad made sure her horse was fed and cared for as well.

A small medium-sized dog with long dark hair was her companion, and it usually ran alongside the horse when she rode from one place to another.

I once went to her cabin and was very surprised and impressed to find her cooking meat bones for her dog to eat. The dogs I knew were fed table scraps or hunted for themselves.

Small differences like that set the missionaries apart and caused them to be labeled as "odd." Some in the local adult religious community didn't take the missionaries seriously.

Once when a local person had said a public prayer that was more conversational and less traditional (without the thees and thous), the resulting comment was, "Oh, he prays like a missionary."

Had it not been for the missionaries, we would not have had the experience of Sunday school, for none was offered at the churches. School Christmas plays and programs were carried out solely by these women, who had the plan, selected the participants, made the costumes, created the props, and provided holiday candy treats. I can almost feel the tinsel halos and taste the grocery mix candy even now.

Miss Lamb, the good woman whose pinky fingers were curled with age and arthritis, was still riding her horse to the one-room schools when we left to live in Cincinnati. Her health declined after a while, and she was no longer in the area by the time we moved back to Kentucky.

By the time we did move back to eastern Kentucky in 1955, Miss Anderson (Lois) had taken Miss Lamb's position. Miss Anderson was a small woman, young, pretty, and serious about her work teaching children about Jesus.

By then, roads had improved and the horse was replaced by a motorized vehicle. No time was wasted as an old retired and donated limousine traveled up and down Johnson Fork, picking up kids for Sunday school and youth activities. The cloud of road dust that billowed high and far behind the vehicle seemed to convey the energy and enthusiasm of the young woman who drove it. The young folks affectionately named the limo Old Many Doors.

Miss Anderson was a talented woman and a devout Christian. She was a good example and mentor. I personally feel that my life was blessed and enriched because Miss Lamb and Miss Anderson came to live on Johnson Fork from an unknown place, representing an unknown earthly group but exhibiting love and commitment to a known and loving God.

Sometime in the '60s, the missionary's cabin accidentally burned to the ground. Miss Anderson single-handedly built a very functional and sturdy block building to replace the cabin, and it stands today as a testimony to her strength, her faith, and her commitment to God, and to the people of Magoffin County, Kentucky.

NORMA PATRICK SETO

Students who attended Turkey Branch School in 1955–1956. Most all of these children attended youth activities and Sunday school, held just up the road at the missionaries' cabin, and were impacted by their good teaching, gentle manner, and love for us.

A TRUE MOUNTAIN MAN

I do not know how John Lee ended up in Sweetwater, Texas, as a soldier in the U.S. Army. It is said that he was so dissatisfied that he left the army and walked the distance between Sweetwater and Turkey Branch in eastern Kentucky. He spent the rest of his life in caves, rock cliffs, and at the end, a log cabin hidden deep in the woods of Magoffin County.

He traded in guns and did minor repairs to guns.

He had a dog named Caper.

John Lee would accept jobs from local people who wanted him to clear a hillside, but with very few exceptions, he would work after dark or before daylight. Because of this, he developed very good night vision.

John Lee was a decent man, but because of the way he lived, he was accused of things that he did *not* do. John Lee would often hide behind a tree or log to hear what passersby had to say about him. In that way, he kept a pulse on the sentiments and opinions held for him within the community.

He was accused of burning Raleigh Patrick's house, and a reward was posted for his arrest. Several men in the community were deputized to help capture him. Most of them were sympathetic to John Lee and would turn the other way or redirect officials when they got warm on his trail.

John Lee's lifestyle made moonshining (whiskey making) the most likely choice for his occupation.

He had no shortage of customers among the men in the community who wanted to imbibe. John Lee's nephew shot John

Lee three times on three different occasions because he wanted to take his moonshine without paying for it. The nephew got his comeuppance when someone shot him in the hip and left him to spend the last years of his life bedridden and invalid. His bad fortune did not alter his bad disposition; he continued to be difficult for the people who tried to take care of him.

John Lee could be generous and welcomed hunters to his cave if a sudden storm came up. He would share his provisions, usually a rabbit or squirrel and hoe cakes, all made on a small iron grate over an open fire. If the bad weather persisted, John Lee's cave provided a fairly warm and dry place for the duration of a storm.

John Lee kept a supply of onions stored in a corner of his cave. Once when he reached to get an onion for cooking, he did not see a small but poisonous snake until it bit him. John Lee survived the bite, but he had a badly swollen hand for a while.

I personally remember John Lee. When we lived on Turkey Branch, we would often hear John Lee walking around the ridges, singing and calling out to his dog, Caper. "Come here, Caper." Since he lived by himself, he had trouble judging how loudly he talked. He could be heard all the way down to the cabin, and the sound echoed around the valleys and hills. It was a lonely and melancholy sound, and it made my mom even more afraid of him. On the other hand, my dad and John Lee were friends, and the two men had a great liking for each other. When Dad mentioned to John Lee that Mom was afraid of him, his response was, "I'd never harm her, and I'd fight anyone else who tried to hurt her." Personally, I believe that to be true.

He once told my grandma, Lucy Belle, that never once was he inappropriate with a woman. However, he did admit that he had seen most of the women in the neighborhood squat to "wet" (his word) in a chimney corner or at the back of their houses or cabins.

My dad's name was McCoy. Most people called him Coy, but John Lee called him Cenoy. I remember well the occasions we would meet John Lee in the woods or, on rare occasions, on the gravel public road. He would ask, "Where ya livin' at now, Cenoy?" He always asked it in a very loud voice.

He would sometimes ask Dad to buy large amounts of sugar for his use in making moonshine. He would say, "You don't know what I'm going to do with this—don't ask—'cause I'm not going to tell you!"

In the later years when John Lee relaxed enough to live in a house (he still chose remote spots), there came a big flood. Dad was concerned for John Lee's safety and well-being. Dad made his way through the flood water to check on him. He found John Lee all right but frustrated at being locked in by the flood water.

John Lee was usually a little braver about coming out of the woods when he was fortified with a little of his own moonshine. On one such occasion, he came to our cabin and asked Mom if he could buy a chicken. Mom, being a little afraid of him anyway and knowing that John Lee always toted a gun, told him yes and that he could simply shoot the chicken of his choice. She remained inside the cabin and instructed him to leave fifty cents for payment on the porch. Normally he was a good shot, but on this day, his aim was a little off because of the influence of the moonshine. By the time he was finished, several chickens lay dead or dying. He placed fifty cents on the porch for the chicken he took. Mom spent the rest of the day preserving (by canning) the rest of the carnage.

Mom is a small woman, fragile and weak-looking by the standard of the hills. One time, John Lee and Dad were working together to clear a field. It was Mom's practice to take water and food to the field sometime in late morning when she knew her man would be hungry and thirsty. On this day, she had a bad cough because of a cold, which did not go unnoticed by John Lee. The next day, out of concern for her, John Lee brought a cough remedy made from his own whiskey and mixed with other things. While Mom appreciated the gesture, she was very reluctant to try it. John Lee had used a leaf stopper to hold the liquid in the bottle, and it was full of bits of leaves and twigs.

Mom's brother Kiser could hold his own with the best or worst when it came to drinking and carousing. However, he had a dramatic change of heart when he accepted Jesus. The last years of his life were given to preaching the gospel and clean living. He showed up at our house one day with a real moral dilemma. He asked Mom whether she thought John Lee should be paid for whiskey he had bought on credit before he became a Christian.

"A debt is a debt," said my mom without hesitation.

Kiser went forthwith and paid John Lee for the whiskey.

WE BECOME TRANSIENT KENTUCKIANS

The goal when we moved to Cincinnati in 1950 was established firmly in their hearts and minds: earn enough money so they could go back to Kentucky with the means to buy a place of their own. Although we lived very frugally in order to save, we always ate well. Mom was a good cook, and Dad never compromised the grocery budget in order to add to the farm fund. But the four of us managed to live for four of the five years in a two-room apartment in a row house on Mulberry Street in Cincinnati, commonly called Over-the-Rhine. The front room was the living room and also the main bedroom. My sister and I slept on one twin bed in the wide hallway that separated the front room from the kitchen. The kitchen was large enough for cooking, eating, playing games, and doing homework. A rollaway bed sat in the corner of the kitchen and was kept there for family members who were just passing through or for others who needed a temporary place to live. Sometimes "temporary" lasted for several months.

Many people moved from eastern Kentucky to Cincinnati during the late 1940s and early 1950s. The *Cincinnati Enquirer* labeled us "transient Kentuckians." At school, we were called hillbillies and laughed at because we "talked funny."

Not long after we moved from Turkey Branch to the apartment on Mulberry Street in Over-the-Rhine, Cincinnati, Mom's brother Kiser and his family came from Kentucky to live in an apartment in the same building. Kiser Jr. (Kidy) and I had been very close since we were babies. With these new circumstances, we became even closer.

We were called names and spat on by neighborhood kids on a regular basis. I remember one day Kidy and I were walking up the street, coming from the store. When the taunting began that day, we had simply had enough. We looked at each other, decided what we had to do, climbed a fence, and took on several kids. They didn't bother the Kentucky cousins much after that day. We were probably eight and nine years old at the time.

Someone gave us a small loom. We figured out how to make potholders, and we sold them to earn money for the movies. Admission was just twenty cents to the Uptown Theater. We generally went there on Saturday afternoons.

Until the day Kidy passed, we would remind each other of those days and how we bonded even more during those trying times. I loved him dearly, and I miss him sorely.

We moved to another very similar apartment just down the street and stayed there for a short time before moving to Lockland.

I went to Vine Street Elementary School for grades two, three, and four and to Lockland School for grade five.

GUNSMOKE SNOOZES

As the years go by, life seems to get busier, as opposed to slowing down as I expected it would.

After an especially busy morning, I will sometimes put all work aside and at one o'clock turn on Memorable Entertainment—ME TV. I settle comfortably on the sofa and allow myself the luxury of a nap while an episode of *Gunsmoke* plays in the background. I enjoy dozing in and out to the sounds of Matt Dillon, Chester, and Miss Kitty solving problems unique to Dodge City and the Old West.

Just recently I had an insightful moment that helps me understand why I enjoy the occasional "*Gunsmoke* nap."

When we moved from the familiar hills of Kentucky to Cincinnati, we lived in a small two-room apartment. With this move, for the first time in my life, we experienced the convenience and power of electricity. The purchase of a new electric-powered radio opened up a whole new world of music and entertainment.

When the day was done and the four of us had settled in bed for the night, the lights were turned off and the radio was turned on. On some nights, I would slip quietly to the foot of my parent's bed, snuggle under the covers near my dad's feet and listen with them to the wonderful programming of 1950s radio. *Gunsmoke* was a favorite. The sound effects created visuals in my mind that played out the stories in great detail. Spurs jingled and footsteps resounded as the characters walked across the wooden sidewalks that were so much a part of the setting of Dodge City.

NORMA PATRICK SETO

THE DREAM BECAME A REALITY!

The Jesse Williams farm was up for sale. The bank account had topped off at $8,500 dollars, which was the asking price for the house and two-hundred-acre farm. Plans were made to finish out the school year, move back to God's country, and take occupancy. When we arrived in early summer, the tenants held fast to their right to stay until their year was up. Not to be delayed once they were ready to come home, Dad and Mom built a rough twenty-by-twenty-foot one-room house in back of the established house, and we lived in that until the agreement was up and the family of renters moved out.

Although enough money had been saved to cover the cost of the farm, there were repairs and improvements to be made. In order to meet those expenses, Dad kept his job as a pipe fitter in Cincinnati. He lived with Aunt Becky for about a year and came home at least every other weekend.

Mom's fear of being alone should not be misunderstood for being timid. She armed herself well against intruders and thieves and was not in the least bit reluctant to step out onto the porch and start shooting. There was pretty strong evidence that a person had been doing night raids to steal corn from our corncrib.

Dad had bought a very long double-barreled shotgun. When he brought it home and sat it in the corner, he advised his petite wife to leave it there because it would deliver a powerful kick if she fired it.

Predictably, one night we heard noises coming around the hill heading in the direction of the corncrib. She grabbed the long gun and some shells. I was usually right behind her, carrying extra shells. My sister was most often under the bed for these episodes. Mom aimed in the direction of the noise (not a good thing to do) and fired. She ended up flat on her back with an injured hand. But … the very next day, we heard the man who was suspect all along was supposedly in bed with tonsillitis. When, out of curiosity, Uncle Vencin went to see him, he returned with the report that no tonsillitis was apparent but the man was moving very gingerly in the bed. He was most likely sore from the buckshot that had landed in his backside just before Mom landed on her backside from firing the gun.

YOU TALK FUNNY!

had lived in the city since I was seven years old. Youngsters make adjustments and pick up new speech patterns very easily and quickly. Now, with the return to the people and the place that I loved best, I was surprised to be facing a challenge similar to the one I had encountered when I went to Cincinnati. They laughed at me because I talked funny! I settled into a way of speaking that was comfortable for me and a little mixed. Please don't judge me on the way that I talk. All those moves in the early years were the cause of it.

It was good to be back in Kentucky. I share my dad's love of the hills and the freedom to roam in the woods. Things had changed on Johnson Fork during the five years we were away. Families had changed, grown, and moved around. Roads had improved. More cars and fewer horses traveled the now-graded road that wound from Route 460 all the way to Linden Fork in Morgan County.

HOME AGAIN!

The move back to Kentucky allowed me to complete my elementary education at Turkey Branch School, and what an education it was! One that I would not alter or trade.

I skipped sixth grade altogether and went right into seventh. Monroe Davis was our teacher. He was middle-aged and somewhat overweight and had habits that didn't necessarily promote good health. Although I never witnessed it, I was told he could fit a regular-sized saucer in his mouth with ease. With the large mouth came a large voice with good volume and memorable quality.

Monroe's first wife had died and left him to raise seven children. After a time, he married a younger woman and they had two lovely daughters, Brenda and Ginger. Ginger was about three years old when she accompanied Monroe to school.

Mom and Monroe were first cousins. I felt a strong kinship with him, as he did with me. For that reason, he was comfortable each day following lunch to say, "Go feed Ginger and clean up my lunch." It was my daily responsibility until very early one morning someone stopped in front of our house and yelled out to my dad, "No school today. Monroe died last night of a heart attack."

Olga Dunn, wife of the county-town undertaker, finished out teaching the school year. She was a tall woman with a pleasant demeanor and voice. Mrs. Dunn was sometimes frustrated by the older boys, who were not always receptive to good teaching and authority, a problem that Monroe had effectively dealt with in his own fashion.

The next year presented a new start with teacher Ethel Morris.

NORMA PATRICK SETO

Mrs. Morris was also from "town." Mrs. Morris was not the least bit intimidated by the boys. Whatever they saw in her eyes when she pulled herself up to her full four-foot-ten height worked to gain cooperation and respect from all of the students.

Mrs. Morris and her husband had a general store in Salyersville, and her lunch included things from the store. Not at all like my lunch pail, which usually held corn on the cob, sausage and biscuit, or jelly with homemade butter. Mrs. Morris and I soon worked out an arrangement that pleased both of us: we traded lunches. Vienna sausage and packaged snack cakes were much more appealing to me than the stuff I brought from home and vice versa. In the area of Magoffin County, Vienna was always pronounced V-I-E-E-N-I-E— long *i* and long *e*. In fact, that is the way I still pronounce it when referring to sausages in a can.

Through seventh and eighth grades, I enjoyed a privilege that was given to me by all three teachers. They would assign my lessons, and as soon as I finished my own work, I very often got to teach grades one through five.

THE "REALITY" OF 1950S TV

Grandma, Grandpa, and Uncle Vencin lived at the head of Settlement Branch until Mom and Dad bought the Jesse Williams farm on the main graded (graveled) road of Johnson Fork. The property was actually two homesteads with two primitive but sturdy houses.

Once the deal was made with Jesse, Grandma, Grandpa, and Vencin bought the second house and some of the property from Mom and Dad, with the road marking the dividing line.

Besides being more conveniently located for the store, the county seat, and transportation, the move for them meant that we would all be available to help care for my aging grandparents. Grandpa was practically deaf, and dear Grandma was dealing with advanced dementia or Alzheimer's disease.

Vencin had already moved and established their household before we began the process of moving from Ohio. Our house was occupied by renters who were slow to give up their hold on the place. For that reason, our furniture was stored at Vencin's house. With help from Uncle Vencin and Uncle Chester, Dad built a very rough twenty-by-twenty-foot building in back of the fully occupied main house. We lived in that small one-room structure throughout the summer and into the fall when time was up and the renters finally moved out.

The time came to move our "stuff" into the house "across the creek." Everything, that is, except the TV set. Grandpa had already in his own weird fashion become attached to it, and so it remained in their house.

Not everyone was privileged to have a TV in the 1950s, especially in Magoffin County, Kentucky. Uncle Vencin's household was the very first in the neighborhood to have one.

Color was not an option! Watching *Wagon Train* on a nineteen-inch black-and-white screen was at that time as good as it got.

Reception was difficult because of the high hills. To get a decent picture, special wire had to be purchased and strung up the hillside to the highest point possible. The wire was then connected to a large antennae, which was mounted on a tall tree at the very top of the hill.

The antennae direction was important and had to be adjusted just right in order to pick up the signal coming out of Huntington, West Virginia.

If only one person was working to get the job done, it required several trips up and down the steep hill to see if there was clarity on the screen. It wasn't unusual to feel really confident in the adjustment only to discover upon your descent a snowy screen and no picture.

Sometimes several people would be recruited and stationed at intervals between TV and antennae. Results of the adjustments could then be relayed along the route to report a good picture or snowy screen.

Even then, a strong wind on the antennae or a fallen tree or branch across the wire could void out all the hard work and the process would have to be repeated. It was difficult to keep TV, wire, and antennae in sync and working well.

Mom revealed to me that once my sister and I left home and there were no youngsters around to form a line, they got a little more creative with signaling. If the picture was coming in well, she would step out onto the porch with her handgun and fire three rounds, signaling success to the person at the top of the hill.

Once everything was working well, the serious TV watching could begin.

I would sometimes camp out at Vencin's in the afternoon to watch *Pinky Lee* or *Howdy Doody*.

Grandpa mostly watched in the daytime. He was especially intrigued by the Westerns, which were so common at that time. He believed the scenarios were real and that the people on TV could see him and interact with him. Dad once walked into the room to find Grandpa in front of the set with a loaded shotgun draped across his lap. A troublesome neighbor had encouraged Grandpa to shoot back if the cowboys started shooting at him.

Another neighbor liked to tell how he once visited to find that Grandpa had put a bucket in front of the TV to catch the horse manure he believed would eventually land on the floor.

Every single evening, a great many people would gather in front of that TV and watch from seven o'clock to nine thirty or ten o'clock. Occasionally adults would show up, but the crowd mostly consisted of young boys. Sometimes as many as twenty would crowd into the small room, which was also Uncle Vencin's bedroom.

We didn't do living rooms in those days. There was a front room and a lower room, and each functioned as a sleeping room furnished with one or two beds. When all available chairs were taken, several people sat or squatted on the floor. It was kind of an unspoken courtesy that nobody ever sat on the bed.

Once we were settled into our own place, Dad bought at least two more TVs at different times. Being the "horse trader" that he was, he either sold them or traded them before he got home with them. And so, each evening we continued to walk down the lane, cross the foot log (foot bridge), and go over the gravel road to watch our TV at Uncle Vencin's house, crowding uncomfortably in with all the boys in the neighborhood. I felt very fortunate, indeed, when everyone had chosen their spots and I ended up sitting next to Kenneth.

NORMA PATRICK SETO

COUNTY NURSE AND COLD FEAR

The county nurse visited Turkey Branch School about twice a year. Tension and cold fear ran high on the days Mrs. Gardner arrived with her large black case. Mrs. Gardner was a pleasant woman with short dark hair. Her navy blue uniform, nurse's cap, and sensible black shoes gave credence to the serious nature of her work. My memories of her are colored by the fact that I got a shot on the occasions of her visits. It was difficult to see beyond the circumstances to understand that Mrs. Gardner truly cared about us and was simply doing what was necessary to keep us healthy.

Mrs. Gardner was usually accompanied by an assistant. In retrospect, it becomes clear in my mind that the assistant's most important contribution was to run down and catch the students who resisted being vaccinated. I saw it happen several times. The most vivid memory is of a blond-haired girl running full speed around the schoolhouse, with the assistant to Mrs. Gardner in hot pursuit. The assistant always got her gal or guy!

THE UNWELCOME BEDFELLOW!

Wildlife was varied and plentiful. Some critters were hunted and useful for food, while others were hunted and eliminated because they were a nuisance or a threat. Many small animals were neither, and they simply existed without interference from humans. Because of the nocturnal nature of the possum and its nonintrusive ways, it didn't get a lot of notice until once in the middle of the night, I woke to see a large drooling possum being held over the bed where my sister and I slept.

Good friend and prankster Billy Tyler worked in Cincinnati and came back home to Kentucky on weekends, usually passing our house on Johnson Fork in the wee hours. As he neared our house on one particular night, he saw a fat possum in the road, apparently stunned by the car headlights.

Billy quickly formulated his evil plan, jumped out of the car, and caught the possum by the tail. My dad was not only a good sport for having been woken in the middle of the night, but he aided Billy by turning the light on just at the right moment so we could actually see the slobbering possum as Billy held it briefly over our heads before dropping it into bed with us.

Was there payback? Oh yes, but I will save that story for another day.

JOBS AND JUICE

I was eleven years old when we finally moved from Cincinnati back to Kentucky.

Once the family was settled "across the creek," Dad began the commute to his job in Cincinnati. He kept working as a pipe fitter for at least a year. He made an effort to come home every other weekend. Because he did not have a car, he was dependent on others who might be returning to Magoffin County. When no rides were available, he rode the Greyhound bus to get home.

His absence left Mom with the responsibility of managing livestock, crops, and household with the help of an eleven-year-old girl and a fourteen-year-old girl.

My sister was very much an inside person, happy to do a little housework and a lot of reading. I, on the other hand, loved the outdoors. I was happy to get back to Kentucky and the freedom to roam in the woods. I was also glad to do any job that required me to be outside. I gathered eggs, fed and watered chickens, brought the cows from the hills for milking, drew water from the well to keep the drinking water bucket filled, and also brought in water to keep the stove reservoir filled. The old-fashioned woodburning stoves had a reservoir on the right side for holding warm or hot water. When the stove was in use, the water would get very hot. The stove was usually fired up at least twice daily, which meant hot to warm water was readily available for washing dishes or clothing or for taking sponge baths.

Hogs were kept in a pen. They ate everything that grew inside their space, leaving it bare of any vegetation. They were always hungry and eager to eat the slop or corn that was added to their rough wooden trough. After all that, they were still hungry. In summer, horse weeds grew tall and plentiful. Every day I would seek out a good spot, cut armloads of the tall itchy plants, and carry them to the pigpen. The pigs ate as if they had not been fed at all. Giving them green weeds made me feel like I was providing a very special treat.

It was also my job to carry in coal for the fireplace. Sometime in the early fall, Mom or Dad ordered a load of coal, which was delivered by truck and dumped in a large heap at the back of the house. Most chunks were easy to pick up and carry in a bucket, just the right size for burning in the fireplace. Some came in large chunks or blocks that had to be broken up, or split, before they were usable.

Just a little aside: Winters were cold, and the entire house was heated by the small grate fireplace. The coal fire was kept burning all day and well into the night. I remember having to deal with the black soot that formed around my nostrils and came out on the hanky when I blew my nose.

Wood fueled the cookstove, and we would sometimes bring fallen trees and branches in from the hills. There was a sawmill about a mile down the road, and it provided another source of wood. Before trees were trucked from the sawmill to a buyer, they were trimmed and dressed. There was always an ample supply of trimmings or slabs sold to locals for a very nominal price. Sometimes log sections were available. The log sections were the right length for burning, but they had to be split into sticks that would fit into the stove. Splitting the logs required the use of a heavy double-blade ax and sometimes the added use of a wedge and a sledgehammer. A log might produce twenty sticks of stove wood when properly split.

Even though I was a slight eleven-year-old, I learned to swing an ax or a sledgehammer to provide wood and coal to keep the fires burning.

However, I did occasionally get a break from this chore.

Local boy Rondal Lee Allen was at least ten years older than me. Early on, we formed an odd but comfortable friendship. He nicknamed me Jose, and that was what he called me until the day he died.

Like a lot of young men in the eastern Kentucky culture, Rondal Lee went through a phase of drinking and fighting. He never came to our house when he was fortified with moonshine, but he would most always show up when he was recovering from a wild weekend of "drinking, fighting, and scratching," as Mom would put it.

Not being a drinker myself, I do not understand the craving for certain food or drink when getting past a hangover. On those occasions, Rondal Lee craved Mom's home-canned tomato juice. As long as I provided the soothing juice, he would split wood or break up big chunks of coal. It sometimes took more than one quart to either sooth Rondal Lee or to get the right amount of wood chopped. During those times, we kept up lively conversation, laughed, told stories, and generally enjoyed each other's company. In my mind's eye, I can still see that quart of red juice sitting on a stump and me sitting on another stump while Rondal Lee did my last chore of the day.

Rondal Lee eventually put his wild ways behind him. He married a wonderful girl from the neighborhood. One of his sons became a preacher.

A QUARTER EARNED!

Boys outnumbered girls in the neighborhood at the time by nearly three to one. The six boys in the Stephens family lived nearby, and they spent a lot of time at our house. One of the favorite pastimes when they came around was to sit on the porch and sing from an old gospel hymn book that belonged to Mom. Everybody tried to get a seat on the porch swing first. Somehow you can get good rhythm going when you swing and sing. The singing could go on for hours, and we knew most of the songs in the book. Our voices were strong and loud enough to be heard for at least a quarter mile around.

Dad enjoyed our singing to a point, but after an hour or two he would often give us a quarter to stop.

One day the dog got hold of the song book and ripped it to pieces. Upon discovering the shredded pages, Kenneth said to Mom, "Oh no. The dog has done destroyed our money-making book."

Kenneth Stephens, a front porch singer.

TO SMOKE OR NOT TO SMOKE?

There are so many reasons to thank my Uncle Vencin! For instance, I thank him that I am a nonsmoker.

Vencin and Dad probably took up smoking as soon as they could walk to the barn to tear leaves from the plants drying there for market. When they grew to be adults, Prince Albert was the brand of choice. The red can with the handsome prince pictured on the front fit nicely into the breast pocket of a shirt.

Vencin's first vehicle was a used Jeep brought to him from Ohio by his brother-in-law, Harkes Johnson. I accompanied Vencin on many trips to the store and into town. Driving along the curvy, gravel mountain roads of Magoffin County took concentration and didn't leave a hand free for making a cigarette when he felt the nicotine urge. Vencin soon learned that with just a little instruction, his young passenger could roll his smokes as well or better than he could do it himself. Still can!

Of course, new things become available even to people living in isolated areas. Sometime in the '50s, Vencin discovered ready-made menthol Kool cigarettes. He didn't buy them on a regular basis but treated himself occasionally to a smooth package of those long, white ready-made sticks.

Once when he had just bought a pack, I was looking on with admiration as he drew one out and lit up. He glanced toward me and asked, "Wanna try it?" Oh yes, no question about it. I eagerly held out my hand to take the lit cigarette. "No wait," Vencin said. "First, I'll tell you how to do it. Now, take a long draw, and before you let it out, suck in your breath as deeply as you can."

I followed his instructions to a tee … and then the room started to spin. I have never had the desire to smoke another cigarette. Vencin knew exactly the result his instruction would get. Tough love? Yeah. But it worked to keep this person from developing a killer habit.

Regrettably, Vencin died in 1986, at age sixty-nine, of lung cancer.

NURNALENE! NURNALENE! NURNALENE!

Uncle Logan was one of Dad's brothers who remained in Kentucky and spent most of his life on Settlement Branch, just about a mile down the branch from his mam and pap. He was an intelligent man. Although he had no formal education, he had an appetite for learning. In his youth, he studied and completed the books of a friend who was fortunate enough to go to high school.

Log (Logan) was a soldier in World War II, and he was involved in very active combat. He returned from the war with physical injuries and shell shock, which in today's world is called post-traumatic stress disorder. Unfortunately, he relied heavily on alcohol to help him deal with the effects the war left on his mind and body. Although he loved his family, his personal choices made life very difficult in many ways for his wife and five children.

We often passed their house on the way to Grandma's, and we always stopped to talk and rest for a while.

Aunt Tressie liked trinkets, and she kept the windowsills lined with Cracker Jack toys. Except for those pieces, there was no color on the house and surrounding small buildings and no evidence that any had ever been painted. The images of those splashes of color remain very clear in my mind, and it is nice to remember that she got joy from her window display. She had a difficult life.

Playmates were few and far between for some of us, so when Log's kids saw me coming, they would set up a chant: "Nurnalene, Nurnalene, Nurnalene!" Oh yes, my full name is Normalene. And when Mom or Dad were ready to leave, on at least one occasion, my cousins hid me under the porch.

Up to the day he died, my cousin James would start the chant—"Nurnalene, Nurnalene, Nurnalene"—each time we saw each other!

DRUNKEN DIGGERS!

Uncle Log had several drinking buddies, and among them was a man named Ernest.

Ernest and Log were together one day, just getting into their cups and discussing the death of a man on the creek. "On the creek" can be substituted for "in the neighborhood." Because the man was well thought of, it was likely there would be a good turnout of local men to help dig the grave. Log and Ernest wondered if, at their demise, anyone would show up to dig their graves.

After another drink, Log told Ernest rather sadly that he knew people didn't care about him and that when he died, he was certain nobody would show up to dig the grave. Likewise, Ernest expressed his doubt that his own death would bring out any gravediggers at all.

Pretty soon, as the drinking progressed, they were sobbing at the prospect of having nobody show up to dig their graves. And then they made a pact. They promised each other that whichever one died first, the other would be there to carry out the task of digging his friend's grave.

Years passed and Uncle Log developed cancer, suffered long, and eventually died. At the time, it was still customary for friends and neighbors to dig the grave. Not only was Ernest the first one there, but he stayed all that night through heavy rain to scoop water from the grave once it was dug so that the coffin of his friend would not rest in water.

A promise made in a drunken stupor … *kept*!

CHURCH ONCE A MONTH

Andy Crase, my maternal grandfather, was a circuit-riding preacher, and Mount Zion Baptist Church was one of the churches he pastored. Each week of the month, he would ride his horse to a different community church, always accompanied by his faithful dog named Judge.

Until recently, the practice of having Sunday service only once each month remained the norm for most of the country churches in Magoffin and Morgan Counties. However, with better roads and means of transportation, the members of one church would attend the other three churches. What's more, some people who have moved to Ohio and other states make their way back each month to attend the church of their youth.

NEW CLOTHES

Grandpa Crase would not solicit or accept pay for any pastoral service. His family existed on what they could produce in the fields. The animals they raised provided meat, milk, eggs, and wool. Grandma made sure clothing was clean, in good repair, and adequate for warmth, but their wardrobe was not overflowing with fashion choices. One day preacher Andy (Grandpa) rode by a farmer's field and saw a scarecrow. Upon noticing that the scarecrow was better dressed than him, he got off his horse and forthwith traded clothes with the frightful fellow. Such behavior also gave him honest fodder for pulpit humor.

FEEDING ON THE FLOCK AND FEEDING THE FLOCK

At some point, the small congregations of the United Baptist churches were organized into the Mount Zion United Baptist Association. Once a year, representatives from each local church would make their way to the "socation" meeting, which was held at a location randomly chosen and located somewhere in eastern Kentucky. In the early years, most of the representatives traveled by horseback or by wagon to attend meetings of the governing body of believers.

On one occasion, Grandpa (Reverend Andy Crase) was traveling to represent the four small churches he pastored as a circuit-riding preacher. It was a long ride on horseback from Magoffin County to Knott County, which was where the meeting was being held this particular year. It was likely Grandpa's mind wandered to many things as he rode his horse past farms and homesteads. For one thing, feeding all the people who gathered for the meeting was always a consideration and required thought and planning. Most participants were far from home, and there were few eating establishments in those days.

As he passed by one farm, he saw a sizable "flock of sheep" grazing in a field. When he spotted the owner of the sheep, he approached and asked if he could take a sheep for the purpose of "feeding the flock" of believers. The farmer agreed. Whether the sheep was donated by the farmer or Grandpa paid for it is not known, but it is certain that he rode away with a fine fat sheep securely held in a canvas bag. Meetings lasted a few days. The story goes that the sheep was slaughtered on Friday, and the gathering of people had a very tasty mutton meal on Saturday.

POOP IN THE PULPIT

Grandpa could always count on a church family to give him lodging when he rode in on Saturday evening in order to be there for a timely service on Sunday morning. Usually the same families accommodated him, and he fell into a comfortable routine, especially with the Harlen Back family.

Each month he rode into the Back family barn, unsaddled his horse, and did a little grooming before offering it feed and water. He carried his Bible in a saddlebag and he hung the saddlebag on a nail that was driven partly into a post at the corner of the stall. He usually arrived just before supper with enough time to wash up after the long ride, which typically took him over hilly terrain and through all manner of weather.

Grandpa was self-taught, ever ready to deliver a fire-and-brimstone sermon or a message of hope and encouragement, whichever the Spirit led him to do. He relied heavily on the leading of the Holy Spirit in all his ministry. And so, on this particular occasion and others, he felt no need to take the saddlebag and Bible into the house with him. In fact, he thought no more about it until the next morning when he slung it over the horse's back and headed for church. When the service had advanced to the sermon, Grandpa stood confidently in the pulpit and opened the saddlebag to get his faithful standard, the Bible.

I wish I had been there to see the look on his face when he opened the flaps to find both sides of the saddlebag filled with horse manure.

He stood for a moment, pointed his finger at Harlen Back, and said, "Harlen, I've never seen such a family as yours. Such fine

Christians on a Sunday that if the Lord comes back today, you'd all go to heaven. But you are all so bad at any other time, if the Lord comes back in the middle of the week, not one of you has a chance!"

That remark was doctrinally unsound for his belief and denomination, but it made everybody laugh and certainly got their attention.

Alonzo Craft, Harry Mullins, and preacher Andy Crase. All baptisms were done in the creek in all types of weather.

A NOSE DRIP

Andy most often rode alone to preach at the four mountain churches that he pastored throughout Magoffin and Morgan Counties. Those churches held services only once a month on rotation. To get the most out of their assigned weekend, churches held services on Saturday afternoon as well as Sunday morning.

Revivals were different in that there were nightly services Monday through Friday, sometimes lasting three weeks. According to Mom, a revival held at Christmastime was a significant part of celebrating the birth of Jesus. For revivals, as well as weekends, lodging was provided for the circuit-riding preachers by a volunteer family from the congregation. Revivals drew in preachers from surrounding counties, and each one of them was given ample time in the pulpit.

Preacher Alonzo Kraft usually showed up for revivals. Alonzo and Andy were good friends. They enjoyed any opportunity for fellowship and to share stories and ideas, and they made an effort to share meals and lodging when they showed up at the same church for a revival.

They had just settled at table and were being served a good meal by their hardworking hostess when one of them noticed a "drip" on the tip of the woman's nose. Andy leaned toward Alonzo and whispered, "Do you think you want to stay here tonight?" Alonzo replied, "It depends on where the drip falls."

SOOTY SOCKS AND SACRAMENT

Grandpa Andy took care of all the duties expected of a preacher. He married 'em, baptized 'em, and buried 'em.

He was also self-taught in other areas. The community depended on him for spiritual advice and direction, legal advice, and help drawing up deeds and correspondence. He also pulled teeth and set bones. He was helpful and usually responded well to all that was asked of him in the community and in the county.

However, he allowed and expected to be served and taken care of when he was at home. He called me Baby, and I can remember him demanding, "Baby, get me a glass of water." Whoever was in earshot or nearby when he had a need was pulled into service. Only once that I know of did his expectations and dependence on family backfire on him.

United Baptist churches follow the loving and serving example that Jesus set at the Last Supper by washing each other's feet. Another story (in this book) mentions that women washed the feet of women and men washed the feet of men. Foot washing usually happened at a Saturday service.

Once, Grandpa Andy was getting ready to go to one of the churches where the foot-washing ritual was to be observed. As his son Kiser passed through the room, Andy, in his typically commanding voice, told Kiser, "Bring me my black socks." No please or any courtesy was remembered. Kiser, though accustomed to this kind of interaction, saw an opportunity as he passed the heating stove. He retrieved the socks from a drawer. Hmm, they were black! Soot is black! He scooped some soot from the stove and dusted the inside of the black socks with black soot. Without suspicion or hesitation, Andy slipped the socks onto his feet and put his shoes on. There was no discomfort or cause to think about his feet until it was time for Andy to remove the shoes for the foot washing. I imagine there was a reaction when the men looked at the feet and wondered not just what was going on but whether they wanted to be the one to wash those feet.

Andy simply said, "That's my son Kiser, just playing a prank!" This was a calm reaction at church, but it is likely Kiser suffered Andy's wrath when he returned home.

RIGHT AS RAIN

The circuit rotation for church was interrupted only in the spring and summer when memorial services were held on family or neighborhood cemeteries. The gatherings were large. Family and friends connected to form large supportive networks or clans.

Once in early spring, Grandpa was preaching a memorial service on a hilltop family cemetery. Suddenly and without warning a spring shower rolled in. The people started to get up from their log seats to scurry down the hill. Never at a loss for words or volume, Grandpa yelled, "*Stop!* You're not made of salt, and you're not made of sugar. Turn around and sit down. This shower will soon pass, and you won't melt." The people turned, sat down, and listened attentively while he finished the memorial message.

Memorial services were almost always followed by "dinner on the ground." Women wouldn't think of bringing just one covered dish to such an event. They brought homegrown and homemade fried chicken, bean dishes, potato salad, berry pies, and berry juice. No one went away hungry. There were always a few freeloaders who failed to bring food but had no misgivings about eating a large share of what others brought. This did not go unnoticed by the women who did all the hard work. Such shameful behavior was talked about and remembered at other functions and then talked about some more.

Those special times gave opportunity to spend time and stay acquainted with all the cousins. I proudly claim fifty-five first cousins, and I can name them all (for the most part) in order of their ages.

TURN THE TABLE

L ucy Belle Elam was the middle child (daughter) of Delilah Lykins and Henry Elam. Emma was the oldest, and Laura was the youngest. Andy was the third child of Peter and Mary Ellen Davis Crase. Rigg was the oldest, then there was Elizabeth (Daught) and Andy, and Jim Henry was the youngest. Their mother, Mary Ellen, died when Andy was only eight years old. It is thought she died of pneumonia after being caught in a rainstorm. After her death, Grandpa Andy was raised by Hoy and Savannah Miller, while the other children remained with their father, Peter Crase.

Life was hard for the ones left in the home without a mother. Andy's host family was better off financially, and he was well cared for and loved by the entire Miller family. Andy once bragged to his brothers that he would one day live in a mansion and would walk "out of the parlor into the hall" to greet them for visits.

Nobody knows the story of Andy and Lucy Belle's meeting or courtship. It is known that her family didn't approve of him as a match for their daughter. He was seventeen and she was sixteen when they eloped in 1902. They had no money and were given no place to live by their families. They moved into a livestock shelter (stable) that had not yet been used for animals. One day as Andy sat outside the shelter, playing his banjo, his youngest brother, Jim Henry, rode up on his horse, leaned toward Andy, and said, "Out of the parlor into the hall looks more like out of the stable into the stall." Andy chased him away, throwing rocks at him until Jim Henry cleared the area.

Andy and Lucy Belle had been married for two years when Morten was born in 1904. Then came Leburn in 1906.

For the first few years, Andy continued to behave like a single man in some ways. He'd go dancing, frolicking, and drinking. Once, after he had been out socializing, he came home and started kicking chairs. He grabbed the table and was about to turn it over when Lucy Belle said, "Wait!" He waited while she gathered all the dishes they owned, put them on the table, grabbed one end, and declared that she was ready to help him turn the table over. He held his end down so that she would not follow through and turn it over herself.

Over the years, Andy took on many responsibilities in the community. Early on, he gave his life to Christ and was ordained to preach at age twenty-four. He was a horse trader and served the community as a dentist, bone setter, vet, legal consultant (a jack-of-all-trades and mostly self-taught). He once ran for county judge and lost by three votes. He taught dancing and music and studied law (on his own). He could never tell his youngest twins apart.

Perhaps of interest only to the family, among the many marriages he performed was the ceremony uniting Denny and Myrtle Elam. Years later, he performed the marriage ceremony of Denny and Myrtle's youngest son.

PUTTING UP WITH PETE

After Peter's first wife, Mary Ellen Davis Crase, died, he married Nanny Craig, who had a family of her own. In Peter's final years, Nanny would send her feeble husband to spend winter months with his son Andy, daughter-in-law Lucy Belle, and their houseful of kids. The expectation was that her aged and cantankerous husband would be cared for from November through March.

Great-Grandpa Pete had a walking stick that had a nail driven into the bottom tip and snipped so the sharpness would give him stability. Never mind the damage it did to floors. Andy's mischievous children would sometimes put the family dog in the room with Pete, and a battle would ensue. Pete would poke the dog and the kids with the nail end of his walking stick.

For the most part, the family catered to Pete. He had his own room in a small house that had to accommodate several other people. On cold snowy days, the children were expected to go outside and around the house in order to get to the kitchen and avoid going through his room. One winter, Grandpa Andy shoveled a path around the house through twenty-four inches of snow just to avoid having the children walk through Peter's room to get to the kitchen.

Pete would deliberately mess his pants and throw them out of his room and onto the floor and demand that Lucy Belle wash and dry them in a short amount of time. She dutifully rinsed the foul clothing in the nearby creek before adding them to the family wash that she did for herself, her husband, and their surviving eleven children.

Peter had developed a pattern of sleeping during the day and expected the adults in the household to stay awake keeping vigil with him through the night.

Any complaint by Peter was addressed by his son Andy without question, explanation, or understanding from the children. Once Peter complained that three-year-old Custer had been making noise and keeping him awake. Andy whipped Custer with a willow switch, leaving welts and stripes on the tender skin of his young back. Upon discovering the incident, oldest daughter Lizie took Custer to Peter's room and forced him to look at the damage he had caused. She pressed Peter up against a wall and informed him that if he caused another child to get whipped, she would personally administer the same punishment to him. He took the threat seriously, and no other child had to endure unjust punishment because of him.

On a more positive note, in his younger years, Peter was a blacksmith by trade. He did business with friends and neighbors, shoeing horses, mending wagons and wagon wheels, and creating and repairing rudimentary farm equipment. It was not surprising that in 1900, he forged a flat iron and gave it to Lucy Belle when she married Andy. The iron has survived for 120 years and is now being used by me as a doorstop in my own house.

Note: Peter Crase came from Virginia.

FAMILY

A ndy and Lucy Belle Elam Crase had fifteen children. Eleven of them survived to adulthood.

Grover and Boyd died in infancy.

Daughter Hazel died at seven, following an accident. She was supporting her weight on two chair backs and swinging between them as children will do. The chairs toppled, and she fell, hitting her head on one of the chairs. At first there seemed to be no cause for alarm. She woke up in the middle of the night, asking for a drink of water. Grandma gave her a drink and was irritated at having been woken in the middle of the night by a whining child. She told Hazel to go back to sleep. Hazel died before morning, apparently from an injury resulting from the fall. For a long time, Grandma struggled with the way she reacted to Hazel that night. There was no way she could have known. Grandma was a Proverbs chapter 31 woman, no question about it, except in her own mind, over that fateful night.

Just two weeks later, Grandma gave birth to a daughter, Savannah.

Beatrice died in the 1918 flu epidemic. The Crase family was exceptional to lose only one child, for that epidemic wiped out entire families in some cases.

Hettie was one of the eleven to live to be an adult. She married at twenty-three and had five children in rapid succession. Without proper medical care and with questionable nutrition, her body was depleted, and with the birth of the fifth child, Hettie died.

She was loved and respected by her siblings. Even though she died before I was born, my mom kept her memory very much alive. She spoke of her so often that her legacy affected my own life. Hettie's children moved away with their father, and contact with their mother's family was infrequent.

When our youngest daughter, Bethany, was in junior high school, she became good friends with a beautiful, energetic, and talented young girl in her class.

On an occasion when Mom was visiting us, we decided to make contact with Hettie's oldest son, who we discovered lived nearby in Loveland. We called and invited the family over. It was a warm and happy reunion for all of us, especially for Mom and her nephew Mayo, Hettie's oldest son.

Just as they were getting ready to leave, Mayo remarked that his granddaughter had been at our house just the week before for a cast party. That is how we learned that Bethany's wonderful school friend was also the great-granddaughter of the very beloved Hettie, my mom's sister.

God is good!

Before cold weather set in each fall, Grandpa would sell a cow and buy each child a pair of shoes with the proceeds.

> Who can find a virtuous woman? for her price is
> far above rubies.
> The heart of her husband doth safely trust in her,
> so that he shall have no need of spoil.
> She will do him good and not evil all the days of
> her life.
> She seeketh wool, and flax, and worketh willingly
> with her hands.
> She is like the merchants' ships; she bringeth her
> food from afar.
> She riseth also while it is yet night, and giveth
> meat to her household, and a portion to her
> maidens.
> She considereth a field, and buyeth it; with the
> fruit of her hands she planteth a vineyard.

NORMA PATRICK SETO

She girdeth her loins with strength, and
strengtheneth her arms.
She perceiveth that her merchandise is good: her
candle goeth not out by night.
She layeth her hands to the spindle, and her hands
hold the distaff.
She stretcheth out her hand to the poor; yea, she
reacheth forth her hands to the needy.
She is not afraid of the snow for her household: for
all her household are clothed with scarlet.
She maketh herself coverings of tapestry; her
clothing is silk and purple.
Her husband is known in the gates, when he
sitteth among the elders of the land.
She maketh fine linen, and selleth it; and
delivereth girdles unto the merchant.
Strength and honour are her clothing; and she
shall rejoice in time to come.
She openeth her mouth with wisdom; and in her
tongue is the law of kindness.
She looketh well to the ways of her household, and
eateth not the bread of idleness.
Her children arise up, and call her blessed; her
husband also, and he praiseth her.
Many daughters have done virtuously, but thou
excellest them all.
Favour is deceitful, and beauty is vain: but a
woman that feareth the Lord, she shall be praised.
Give her of the fruit of her hands; and let her own
works praise her in the gates.

—Proverbs 31b: 10–31 (Kings James Version)

Preacher Andy and his wife, Lucy Belle Elam Crase.

NO MORE STRIPES

Grandpa Crase once told five of the Crase children to hoe the corn on a hillside field. For no apparent reason, he instructed them to start hoeing at a certain end of the field. Not understanding his reasoning and seeing no difference in where to start, they decided to begin hoeing at the opposite end of the field, which was more expedient.

Savannah was the exception; she knew to follow Grandpa's instructions without question. He was a harsh disciplinarian.

Upon seeing that Mom, Kiser, Les, and Custer had not followed his direction, Grandpa came to the edge of the field and stood waiting at the bottom of the hill. He called for them to come down to take their punishment for being disobedient.

The boys took their lashings from the long willow switch. They stood bravely for their punishment. Mom was the last in line and looked on as her brothers were whipped. When it was her turn, she timidly stepped forward. On the third lick, she opted to run ... and run she did. Grandpa wasn't big on physical exertion and did not pursue the runaway. He stood and kept yelling, "Max, you get back here." As she ran up the hill, she called back, "If you want me, come and get me." He turned and walked back to the house.

The five children went back to work and finished the field. The work went slowly because they were sore and unhappy and they wanted to avoid their dad for as long as they could.

When they finally showed up for supper, Grandma recognized a problem. She took Mom into the kitchen to examine her and treat the stripes made by the three severe lashes of the willow switch.

Grandma rarely confronted her husband, but when she used a certain tone of voice, Grandpa knew to pay attention. She commanded him to come see the result of his bad judgement and harsh discipline. He looked at Mom's back and then turned and walked away without a word.

He never used a switch to discipline Mom again.

CONFIDENT!

When he was only seventeen years old, Mom's younger brother, Les, went to Cincinnati to look for work. He applied for a job at Fox Paper Company in Lockland, Ohio. In an interview, he was asked if he could do mechanic work. He had limited experience working with his brother-in-law in a garage, where he helped to repair cars, trucks, and small farm equipment. In spite of never having seen a machine as big and as complex as the one that would be his first repair project, Les replied, "Yes. I can do anything." He was hired and asked to report for work the following day.

He completely and painstakingly disassembled the machine, laying the parts out in a way that would allow him to put it back together whether he was able to fix it or not.

After three weeks, he had identified the problem, made the repair, and reassembled the machine, thus securing his place as a top mechanic with the Fox Paper Company.

One evening after work, Les had a massive heart attack and died at the age of thirty-three. He was well liked for his good nature and outgoing personality. He was highly respected for his natural ability as a mechanic.

SHE HATH DONE WHAT SHE COULD

randma (Lucy Belle Elam Crase) gave birth to fifteen children. The last pregnancy produced twin girls. In raising all those children, she had to rely on her good instincts and methods passed down from her own mother, who was a midwife and herb doctor. Treatments for childhood ailments were interesting, creative, and worthy of mention for historical purposes if not for effectiveness. Though not recommended today, some of the methods were effective and should not be disputed.

Earache is a common problem with children, both then and now. When one of the Crase kids complained of ear pain, Grandma collected goose poop, added water, boiled it down, strained it, and dropped the resulting liquid into the infected ear as a treatment.

Chamber lye is boiled down human urine and was also used to treat earache. Once, the youngest boy's cry because his ear was hurting was keeping the others awake. The next oldest brother decided to skip the middle steps of preparation (boiling down) and simply peed in his brother's ear to shut him up so that the rest of the household could get some sleep.

Cigarette smoke blown into the ear was also used as temporary relief for earache. The pressure of blowing into the ear probably gave more positive results than the smoke.

Sweet tobacco (Brown Mule) was given as a poultice for toothache, which could explain why some people developed a tobacco habit at an early age.

A handful of boiled sow bugs administered two to three teaspoons at a time was said to be good for bole hives in babies.

Cooked squirrel and squirrel gravy is the cultural equivalent of a Jewish mother's hot chicken soup. When there was sickness in the community, some compassionate woman would cook a squirrel, make gravy with the juices, and deliver the whole thing to the afflicted person. My mom still does this if she can get the main ingredient from a squirrel hunter.

With such a large family to provide for, Grandma not only had to be very diligent in planting and harvesting a garden, but she also needed to plan and grow enough produce to last through the winter months. She prepared the vegetables and put corn, beans, etc. into large wooden barrels filled with brine. After a while, a thick blanket of mold would grow on the top. When one of the children was tasked to get food from the barrels, they were always reminded to carefully lift the blanket of mold, or "mother," retrieve enough vegetable for a meal, and then just as carefully fold the "mother" back over the top because it helped preserve the food, keep insects away, and keep the food from rotting.

Many foods could be dried, sulfured, or canned. Pumpkins and apples were commonly dried. Pumpkin was cut into strips and hung on a rack to dry. Apples were peeled, cut into sections, spread on feed sacking, and left to dry in the sun. Mom continued to dry apples in the open air until in recent years she discovered the process could be sped up and insects kept away if she put them in the back window of her car.

Sulfuring apples preserves them well and gives them a unique flavor (when cooked) that is unmatched in my experience. The apples maintain their color and firmness when they are preserved with sulfur. I've watched Mom do it many times. She began with a clean churn and then placed the apples loosely inside until the churn was about two-thirds full. A small shallow ceramic bowl was used to hold a few wads of cotton topped with sulfur. The sulfur was lit and the churn and its contents were covered with a blanket or quilt to hold fumes inside. After the sulfur burned out, Mom would remove the cloth and store the apples in large one-gallon glass jars.

Lucy Belle Elam Crase was a good wife and mother, longsuffering and humble. Her daughter Maxine remembers when she was paid tribute by a neighbor for keeping fire all year round. Other women would come to her for live coals to restart and keep their own fires going.

GAGGING AT GREAT GRIMY GUTS

It was hog killin' time when the weather turned cold in October or November. For months the hogs were fattened on corn, slop (table scraps and dishwater), and plenty of fresh water.

All parts of the pig were preserved in various ways and used for some good purpose. The head, ears, and other variety meats were used to make souse meat. Meat made into sausage was fried and then canned. Shoulders and hams were salted or smoked and hung in the smokehouse to season. Feet were sometimes pickled.

Lucy Belle used the intestines or guts to make lye soap. Before they were acceptable for use in soap, they had to be cleared of feces, or pig poop. The girls in the family were assigned the job of squeezing the guts until they were free of any visible waste. They were then hauled to the creek, washed several times, and rinsed several times. Back at the house, they were washed and rinsed until odor could not be detected. The girls worked hard at the task, but they would frequently have to turn their heads away to gag.

The guts were then put into a cast-iron kettle, to which was added a can of Banner Lye and at least a gallon of water. The kettle was placed over an outside fire, stirred occasionally, and allowed to simmer until the soft tissue was dissolved by the lye. It was important to stand far enough away so that the toxic fumes didn't get into the lungs.

The kettle and its contents were set aside to cool and solidify. The soap was cut into squares while it was still slightly warm. The squares were then lifted out and set on a board. After several days of drying, the soap was ready for use in washing clothes, shampooing hair, cleaning floors, and any other job that required soap. The lye soap was very effective in getting clothes clean and bright. When used as a shampoo, it made hair very soft and shiny.

Once the job was complete, the strong smell of guts and pig poop lingered on the hands. Aunt Lizie came up with a method that seemed to work well to neutralize the smell. The family had corn bread almost every day. When the cornmeal was sifted for bread making, there was always a handful of bran left in the sifter. In keeping with the idea of "nothing goes wasted," the bran was saved and used as a deodorizer. A small amount of corn bran placed in a pan was set on fire. Holding your hands over the fire and smoke from the corn bran was effective in ridding the hands and forearms of the barnyard smell.

PLEASE PLACE A ROSE ON MY GRAVE

Eliza Crase was the oldest daughter of Andy and Lucy Belle Crase. She was a beautiful young woman who had many suitors, but she was very particular and did not find her prince until she was twenty-three years old. Back then, to be single at that age qualified her as a spinster.

One of her admirers was a handsome, healthy, and strapping fellow named Ollie Davis. Ollie was good-hearted and helpful. When Grandpa was away, Ollie could be counted on to come through deep snow to chop and carry wood in to keep the Crase family's fireplace and cookstove well supplied.

He was not easily discouraged by Lizie's lack of interest in him. He continued to visit with intent to court her, but she stood her ground and did not respond to or encourage his attention. At some point, reality set in for him, and he seemed to have come to terms with her lack of affection for him. However, he did ask one favor of her, which once promised seemed to satisfy him for all time. He asked that upon his death and burial, she place a rose on his grave. Did he have a premonition? Nobody knows. But within a short time, Ollie Davis died of a gunshot. He was ambushed on Cow Creek. A shootout ensued, and Ollie was the only one to lose his life.

Aunt Lizie was still a single woman at the time. She remembered the promise to place a rose on his grave but was concerned that the neighbors would gossip and speculate about their relationship. At that time, a girl's reputation was protected and valued.

After discussing the dilemma with her mother, Lucy Belle, it was decided that Aunt Lizie would select a rose, give it to her mother, and her mother—accompanied by Lizie—would place the rose on Ollie's grave.

The Crase family continued to place a rose on his grave at regular intervals for many years.

Lizie married Chester Lovely when she was twenty-four years old.

Eliza Crase Lovely, Mable Perkins (Mrs. Leburn) Crase,
and Hettie Crase Taulbee, circa 1935.

JUDGE NOT!

Janie Perkins was a person who lived up the road from Andy and his family. She was a very early riser, and she had a habit of visiting neighbors early in the morning. One morning when Andy, Lucy Belle, and the family were still sleeping, they were awakened by a steady *tap-tap-tap* at the door.

Andy said, "Get up, Lucy Belle, and see who that is at the door this early in the morning." Lucy Belle got up, answered the door, and invited Janie to come in. Grandma was always a sweet and hospitable neighbor.

Aggravated at having to get out of bed so early, Andy very frankly told Janie that she wasn't welcome at that hour and that she was making a real nuisance of herself in the neighborhood. She retorted, "I can do what I want to, Andy, and I'm just glad you're not my God."

Andy, always ready with a quick answer said, "Janie, you'd better be glad that I am not God, because if I was, the neighbors would be saying, 'Janie died last night.'"

PASTORAL PRAYER

Sanford Brown and his wife, Lizzie, walked the two miles from their home on Long Branch to Mount Zion Church. They were elderly. Sanford was thin and very stooped from years of backbreaking manual farm work and working in the coal mines. Lizzie was soft-spoken and shy.

On the Sundays set aside to take communion, the church body would also follow the example Jesus set when he washed the apostles' feet, a practice that for many years was an important part of communion services at Mount Zion Baptist Church.

It is heartwarming to remember Sanford walking down the dusty road with a small basin and towel tucked under his arm in preparation for the humble and loving act of washing the feet of his neighbors and fellow church members. Lizzie usually walked a few paces behind him, carrying her own basin and towel. Women washed women's feet, and likewise, men washed only men's feet.

Once when Sanford was working in a shallow coal mine, a large piece of slate rock fell and trapped his body so that he could not move. Help was summoned to remove the rock. Sanford also asked that his pastor, my Grandpa Crase, be sent for to pray for him. Grandpa arrived at the mine and, upon assessing the risk, said to Sanford, "You pray in there, and I'll pray for you out here." As the men worked to free Sanford, he continued to pray, and Grandpa prayed with him … from the safe vantage of outside the mine.

PEPPERED SNAKES

It was the practice of some religious sects to test their faith by handling poisonous snakes. It was more common several years ago than it is today.

Preachers' kids have always had the reputation for being mischievous and more willing to test boundaries than average children. Mom and her siblings were no exception. In fact, they confirmed the notion repeatedly with their antics.

Once, when a religious group had captured, caged, and planned a snake-handling ceremony, Uncle Les (Mom's brother) and a close friend of his heard about the plan. The two boys snuck into the room where the snakes were being held. They sprinkled the caged snakes generously with black pepper. Any movement by the snakes would then stir up the pepper, causing the snakes to become agitated beyond any possibility for them to be touched.

The snake-handling session was cancelled.

Even though the practice of handling snakes was not one that Grandpa Andy would have endorsed, if he had known Les sabotaged the snake session, Les would have been in very big trouble with his dad, Preacher Andy.

FLUSHING OUT THE FOX!

Preachers' kids are notorious for being mischievous and coming up with creative ways of misbehaving.

One day in early spring, Kiser, Les, Savannah, and Maxine were instructed to clear and plow a hillside for planting corn.

Kiser, being the oldest male, was given the task of plowing, while the other three "sprouted" or cleared the area of small trees, briars, and rocks. They were expected to work hard and usually stuck to the task. But Kiser, after toiling for several hours to loosen the hard ground, decided it was time for a break. He left the plow and ran into the nearby woods, taunting his siblings to give chase.

Pretty soon they were involved in a full-blown game of Fox and Hounds. Kiser, as the fox, was quick and smart. He managed to elude capture at every turn. The other three, growing weary, decided to flush out the fox by setting the woods on fire.

Predictably, the fire spread and got out of control. Neighbors were called and asked to bring shovels, hoes, and rakes to create barriers, thus hoping to contain the blaze.

Many people showed up, including one man who assessed the situation, guessed what had happened, and decided to report his thoughts as "certainties" to Preacher Andy. Of course, the man was right, but the four kids convinced their dad that the fire had come across the hill from an unknown origin.

They lied so well that they escaped punishment. However, the man who told on them did not! He was a contracted mule-carrying mailman, which meant that he had a predictable daily routine. The Crase kids collected and piled rocks for an ambush to be carried out the following day. As the neighbor mailman passed through a narrow creek bed, rocks seemed to come out of nowhere. He had to lean over to one side of his horse to avoid serious injury.

As he galloped away, he heard this warning: "Tell on us again and your punishment will be worse."

PASTORAL PRANK
(LARK ARNETT HILL)

My maternal grandfather, Reverend Andy Crase, circuit-riding preacher, rode horseback over the dirt roads and hollers of Morgan, Breathitt, Magoffin, and Wolfe Counties to attend pastoral duties at four different churches and then some.

On one occasion, he was making his way over the Lark Arnett Hill on Middle Fork when he encountered several men at the top of the hill. Grandpa was asked to carry one of the men off the hill. He agreed and asked the other men to lift the obviously very drunk man up onto the horse. He would ride behind, hold onto the man, and carefully guide the horse down the steep and winding dirt road that was Lark Arnett Hill.

"Oh no," said the men. "You must walk and carry him on your back."

Grandpa was not a timid man, but neither was he stupid. Although he knew some of the men, he sensed a challenge of some sort and he could not be sure of their intent. He was definitely outnumbered.

He dismounted, lifted the man onto his back, and began the long and treacherous walk down the hill. When finally they reached the bottom, the man sprang up, sober and laughing. He was joined by the others to celebrate just one more practical prank successfully played on the good Reverend Andy Crase. It happened a lot!

Just this week I had reason to drive across Lark Arnett Hill. The road is now smooth and blacktopped, but the steep curves and inclines remain just as sharp and long as when Grandpa made his way down with what he thought was a very intoxicated man draped over his shoulders.

TOOTH TRAUMA

Grandpa took care of all the family dental needs.

Les had several baby teeth that had become loose, and Grandpa persuaded him to allow those teeth to be yanked out. He never forced the issue, but he was persistent and usually applied strong pressure until the child was willing.

Someone in the family, possibly Grandpa Pete, had built a small chair for the children in the Crase family. Grandpa coaxed Les into sitting in the chair and instructed him to hold on to the rounds in preparation for extraction of the teeth.

Les followed instruction, and Grandpa pulled the teeth fairly easily, but Les was traumatized and, as Mom puts it, "squalled like a tomcat."

Grandpa, wanting to make a point to Les, said, "Now, Les, watch this."

He then told Mom to sit in the chair, hold on to the rounds, and not raise her hands until he was finished. She had protruding permanent eye teeth that were a bit unsightly. They were called "tushes," which I am guessing was a way of saying "tusks."

He started gently rocking the permanent teeth to loosen them. The first tooth was removed. He instructed her to rest and then said, "We will now get the other one."

After the second tooth came out, she asked if she could get up to get a drink of water. He kept her sitting in the chair for a time before allowing her to get up.

Finally, he gave the okay for her to stand, rest a minute, and go without support from anyone to rinse and get a drink of water. She made it across the room before passing out cold.

By the time she awoke, Andy had realized his mistake and made the decision to ride on horseback to Caney to get advice from Dr. Whitaker, who was a regular dentist.

Not many people were willing to correct or confront the strongminded and authoritative Andy Crase, but Dr. Whitaker told Andy that he should never have pulled those permanent teeth. His reprimand included the strong opinion that it was the craziest thing Andy had ever done.

The doctor sent medicine and supplies back to help stop the bleeding and control the pain. Neighbors Mary Jane and George Crase came to sit up all night with the family. That was customary at times when someone in a family was seriously ill or injured.

By the time she was twenty-three years old, Mom's teeth had deteriorated to the point that she needed dentures. Could the problem have started with that untimely removal of two perfectly good, though protruding, permanent teeth?

INEFFECTIVE ARMY ESCORT

During World War II, many young men from Magoffin, Morgan, and Wolfe Counties stepped up to serve in the armed forces. Some were drafted, others volunteered, and then there were those who felt so strongly about serving that they lied about their age when they enlisted. Patriotism and love of country was strong in the hills of eastern Kentucky.

Mom's older brother Leburn served in Panama during peacetime before World War II broke out. Two of her younger brothers were involved in combat during WWII and fortunately came back alive. Dad's brother Logan also served and came back deeply affected and traumatized by the experience.

Others were not so fortunate. Mom's cousin Sye Crase was among the brave soldiers who lost his life serving in France. When a fallen man was declared dead, the dog tags were placed between their teeth for later identification. The body of Sye Crase was sent home to Morgan County months after the family was notified of his death. The U.S. Army sent an escort with the coffin to ensure it remain closed and sealed because of the deteriorated condition of the body.

Relatives of Sye, particularly his brother Guy, would not be satisfied until he could see for himself that it was really his brother Sye, who would be laid to rest in the Crase family cemetery. He knew if he could see the remains, it would be easy to identify Sye by evidence of a broken arm that happened years before he went to the army.

The Crase men would not be outdone by the U.S. Army or anyone else when it meant making sure it was their brother who was in that box. In their minds, the right to confirm Sye's identity overrode any instruction or authority of the escort accompanying the body.

The escort might have been less than enthusiastic about his assigned detail. He most likely relaxed once the coffin was delivered, and when the Crase family men offered him moonshine, he graciously accepted and settled in to observe the traditional way in which mountain folk grieve the death of a loved one. The Crase men kept the moonshine flowing. Over the next few hours, the escort became so inebriated that he passed out cold.

All was going according to plan.

The coffin could now be opened and the body inspected without interference from the outsider. It was not a pretty sight, but it was felt by all that identification was confirmed by the broken arm and also by the dog tags, which were found where the family had been told they were placed at the time of his death.

I heard these details from an older cousin who was present during most of the events, and I heard the story again from a friend and neighbor who was also there. Neither man remembered if, upon his recovery, the escort realized he had been set up and that the coffin had been opened. In any case, I'm guessing he returned to his regular post and kept his mouth shut.

ALL OVER BUT THE SHOUTIN'

Shouting should not be confused with similar forms of expression in other religious denominations.

I was raised in a denomination that interprets literally the biblical admonition for women to remain silent in church. No woman was ever ordained to preach or teach, and no church office could be filled by a woman. However, it is not unusual to hear and see a woman shout, especially near the end of a highly charged service. Shouting is difficult to describe because it is not officially recognized as part of the service.

Shouting is spontaneous and can erupt when a person, usually a woman, feels especially full or blessed by a church service that includes good singing and preaching. Shouting can go on for several minutes while the rest of the congregation sings near the closing of a service. It is not unusual to have one or more persons shouting at the same time. Shouters usually have the cadence and volume that is similar to old-fashioned preaching. The shouter exhibits rapid talk, a reddened face, free-flowing tears, and raised arms. Content usually takes the form of a testimonial, relating the blessings of God or state of the family, church, community, or world. The shouter also encourages fellow church members to pray. If the shouter continues beyond the completion of the service, the congregation stands, waiting patiently and prayerfully until the shouter slows down and works her way back to the pew. Hence, the expression, "It's all over but the shoutin'!"

THE REAL MCCOY

My Dad, McCoy Patrick, was the youngest of ten children. It was truly a wonder that he survived infancy. Yellow jaundice and very low birth weight gave him poor odds of living to adulthood. His mother carried him on a small pillow and covered him with a handkerchief to protect him from flies.

Despite receiving no professional medical care, he responded to the tender care of his family. In fact, they pampered and spoiled him and set a pattern that carried into his adult life. Most people who knew him well loved him dearly and continued the pampering.

He had only a fourth-grade education, but he was blessed with a good mind and practical common sense.

Dad loved Kentucky and the simple life.

Some of his farm chores were laborious but did not require a lot of thought and concentration. Dragging a field was just such a task.

In the springtime, the fields were plowed. Most local farmers had a team of two mules. Usually one mule was hitched to a large single-blade plow. The farmer walked behind, guiding the mule and the plow blade one row at a time until the entire field was turned (plowed).

Another pass over the field with usually two mules pulling a disc broke up the large clods of dirt. This equipment was wider and had several round discs that turned together to make this step a little quicker than plowing. Before the final step of furrowing, the field had to be dragged to make it visually flat. Every farm was equipped with a drag.

Drags were simply several wide boards held together by a few boards nailed in the opposite direction. The drag was usually eight to ten feet square.

Only one mule was needed for dragging. The flat drag went smoothly over the plowed and disc-broken soil. The farmer rode on the drag. This step was restful, boring even, but the added weight of the farmer helped flatten the soil in preparation for furrowing and planting. Sometimes a very big rock was added for even more weight.

Dad had been sitting on the drag behind the mule, and on this particular day, was dealing with being behind a mule that had extreme flatulence. Being a bright and analytical person, Dad posited, *If this is gas, I wonder if it will burn like gas.* There was only one way to find out. Dad was a smoker. He took matches from his pocket and waited for his opportunity. The mule didn't disappoint him. When the mule's tail lifted to expel more gas, Dad struck the match and quickly held it near the mule's backside.

Mom describes it best when she tells how shaken and pale Dad was when he finally walked into the house after being dragged through the field, up the hillside, and through the creek by a mule who was frightened so badly at the torch that had unexpectedly flashed from his rear-end.

FAT AND PURTY

A unt Myrtle, oldest sister of my dad, married and moved to Trent Fork in Wolf County, about fifteen miles from her family on Settlement Branch.

Whether a person chose to travel through the hills on foot or by horseback around the wagon road, the journey took almost a full day.

In the early years of her marriage, visits home were rare. In fact, I got to know her better only after roads improved and transportation became more available. I value the close relationship with her that began when I was about twelve years old. She would have been fifty-four.

The road up Trent Fork is very narrow. Since the '60s, it has been graded and graveled. Its course follows the old wagon road, which runs around the base of the hills, sometimes climbing and dipping to avoid streams and preserve precious tendable bottomland. The road, though rough and narrow, is easily maneuvered most of the year in a pickup truck. At one point, there is an incline before the road becomes straight and flat. Trees grow very densely on both sides and meet together at the top to form a long canopy that is beautiful at any season.

Until she died at eighty-eight, I made a practice of visiting Aunt Myrtle when I returned to eastern Kentucky. By the time I grew up, the trip from Mom's on Johnson Fork to Aunt Myrtle's took about half an hour. Most of the time, we drove Uncle Vencin's pickup truck.

Widowed and living alone, she appreciated company, and her ear was tuned to catch the sound of the pickup coming up Trent Fork long before she could actually see it. One bright summer day, we were just coming around the hill into sight when we saw her already running barefoot to meet us.

My children were young and eager to see her and to play with the cats and kittens that scampered freely around her house and outbuildings.

As the truck stopped, I bounced out to embrace Aunt Myrtle. She stood with her arms out and a big smile on her face. With total affection and admiration, she said to me, "Ohhhhh, you're so fat and purty!"

Her honest and practical perspective has helped me over the years to accept the changes that have occurred as my body has grown older and a "little" larger.

AUNT MYRTLE VERSUS
THE GROUNDHOG

Aunt Myrtle was not intimidated by hard work. She and her husband, Dennie, worked together to make a living for their family. Uncle Dennie lost his arm in a sawmill accident, and he relied on Aunt Myrtle to help with the difficult farm tasks, including but not limited to clearing fields for crops and pastures. She was comfortable with caring for livestock. Feeding and milking were part of her daily routine.

She excelled at growing things. Even after her husband died and their children were grown and gone, she continued to grow large amounts of vegetables in gardens all around her house. I remember cabbage heads too big to carry and ripe red tomatoes too plentiful to use.

She freely shared the abundance with friends and family, but her generosity was tested by a fat groundhog who for several years lived just at the upper edge of Aunt Myrtle's largest garden.

In spite of all her efforts to get rid of the groundhog, he continued to live comfortably and grow fat on the "fruit" of her labor.

One day as she worked in the garden, she felt the urge to empty her bowels. Being a modest woman, when she described this bodily function, she would say she needed to "go hockey." She probably considered the distance to the old outside toilet, looked around, and made a quick decision. The groundhog hole was nearby. It was wide and fairly deep. She had privacy. The hole was suitable for the purpose, in the practical sense to relieve her body and in the moral sense as an expression of the frustration the groundhog had caused for so many years. It seemed fitting and served him right. She hockeyed in the groundhog hole!

After she had tended to the business at hand, she picked up her hoe and with relief and satisfaction went back to working in the garden.

What she had failed to do by all other efforts, she accomplished with a very basic bodily function. The groundhog moved out lock, stock, and barrel, never to be seen again.

A SURE CURE FOR SHINGLES

A few years ago, Mom suffered a severe case of shingles on her head and face. The disease invaded her throat, went deep into her ears, and came dangerously close to her eyes. It was a very severe case that, according to the doctor, simply had to run its course, which could take months. At that time there was no known medical cure for shingles.

According to Aunt Myrtle, shingles could be successfully treated and cured by a method that had been passed down to her through generations.

Using the warm blood of a black chicken, one saturates a cloth and applies it freely to the affected areas. The results for Mom were dramatic and impressive. The areas that could be reached with the treatment responded quickly and healed.

Some of the remedies that served her and her family may seem outrageous, but in some cases their effectiveness was unquestionable. (See the appendix for more home remedies.)

Aunt Myrtle was a healthy woman. She had her first physical examination after her eightieth birthday, and even then, she strongly resisted certain aspects of the exam.

KEEPING IN TOUCH WITH COUSINS

Aunt Myrtle was the last survivor of my dad's siblings. After her funeral, the cousins agreed we should make a concerted effort to keep in touch. I took it upon myself to organize a gathering at three-month intervals. Throughout the year, we kept it simple. Most of the time we would have a good turnout just to grab a sandwich at a local restaurant.

The Christmas gathering took a little more planning.

One year, I asked everyone to bring an exchange gift. There was only one guideline for the gift: it had to be something family related and not purchased from a store. Someone took home a bag of nice sweet potatoes. Another person was pleased to get a quart of home-canned pickled beans. I was very happy to be given a cowbell that had functioned for many years to locate the cow on Aunt Myrtle's farm.

Cousin Alton was puzzled about what to bring. He could think of only one thing but didn't know how to present it. I wrote the following description to accompany a CD that he gave in the exchange.

The Mystery of the Trent Branch Rocking Chair

As most people know, I still have a strong attachment to Trent Branch, where I grew up. I like to spend as much time there as I can. It has been my practice in the past to electronically record the night sounds when I'm at the old homeplace. When I come back to Middletown, I can pop in a tape and go to sleep by the old familiar and loved sounds of crickets and owls.

The tape you have been given is just such a recording. The player was set up on the front porch to record night sounds. As I listened to the tape the next morning, I realized I had recorded another sound that was very familiar to me but one I hadn't heard in many years.

After a long day's work, my dad, Dennie Elam, would sit on the front porch to rest and rock away the stress of the day. The sound of his rocking was unique because the rockers had, through much use, become flattened on the bottom. So the sound it produced was a rockety-bump sound.

Now, when you play this tape, listen carefully from beginning to end at the old rocking chair sound I recorded that night. By the way, the rocking chair has not been around physically for a long time.

—Written for Alton Elam by Norma Seto, 1995

EARS LOWERED

Older women seldom cut their hair. Young women wore braids or curls, and older women twisted their long hair a few times and shaped it into a bun at the back, toward the crown of the head.

If a woman or girl chose to cut her hair, a lock was placed outside under a rock for good luck.

I remember being admonished for even considering cutting my hair or trimming my fingernails on a Sunday, for it was strictly forbidden.

Men kept their hair short, but there were no professional barbers in the community. Like so many other services, haircutting was performed by a man who had a sharp pair of scissors or clippers and a knack for cutting hair. For many years, Uncle Vencin was that person on Johnson Fork. Every week on Saturday afternoons, men would show up to get their "ears lowered," as they commonly called a haircut.

In summer, Uncle Vencin would set up in the side yard and cut hair for several hours. No payment was offered or expected for the service. He never knew in advance how many would come for a cut. The men and boys didn't seem to mind the long wait. They happily passed the time talking about crops, politics, religion, or just plain gossiping.

A SUDDEN DEATH

Undertakers' services were not always considered for use when a person died. Up until the late '50s and early '60s, it was not uncommon for a family to forego embalming. The reasons were sometimes religious, sometimes financial, but most of the time simply practical.

Neighborhood men took care of digging the graves. Ed Burton was considered the most skilled and usually directed the task of building the coffins.

Certain people in the community were called upon to take care of the body, or lay the person out. Often Mom would be called upon to minister to a bereaved family in this way. The body was washed, hands folded over the chest or abdomen, and coins placed over the eyes to keep them closed. A strip of fabric was wrapped around the head, from under the chin to the top of the head. This was to keep the mouth closed and to prevent the jaw from setting slack.

I was favored by a childless couple called Raleigh and Asenith (Sinny) Patrick. I loved them, and they often asked me to spend time with them. Sometimes I stayed overnight, and they treated me like the child they never had. They ran a very small country store. Folks would come to patronize the store and to catch up on the news and politics of the time.

One day, very suddenly a patron of the store dropped dead and fell right off the end of the porch. The body was carried into the room in which I normally slept on my visits. Mom was sent for to lay the body out, in this case, just until the undertaker could arrive.

I walked by the room and saw the body lying on the bed. The

late afternoon sun came through the window and reflected eerily off the coins over his eyes. His hands were folded and his jaw was tied up with a rag. I knew at that moment I would not be sleeping in that room again. I never explained to Raleigh and Sinny. They never knew the reason my overnight visits stopped. I always came up with a good excuse, and the memory of that day has not faded from my mind.

WHEN A BODY "LAID A CORPSE"

few women, including Mom and Mary Louise Dunn, were often called upon to sew the burial shroud and create the lining of a coffin. The women usually worked in teams of two, sometimes sewing all night to complete their work. Coffins were padded and lined with good fabric. The women had their own techniques for sewing and pulling threads to make the gathers and tucks that gave the body a respectable and peaceful resting place.

A body that had not been embalmed was usually "kept up" not more than forty-eight hours. Even then, small bags of salt were placed over the body but under the shroud to preserve the body and prevent discoloration.

When the body was ready, a room was cleared of everything but chairs and the coffin. Friends and neighbors came prepared to sit up all night offering sympathy and sharing stories of the deceased. Family members could steal away for a short rest, but the body was never left without someone in attendance.

Young folks went along out of respect but also to seize the opportunity to stay up all night with their friends. To allow adults space in the room where the body lay, anyone under twenty-one usually gathered in a separate room. We were always admonished to keep the noise at a respectable level. Shamefully, I remember some of the best and most fun times were had when a body "laid a corpse."

POSSUM TRACKS

Have you ever had an unexplainable sensation of cold that comes on very quickly and gives you goose bumps? Mountain folks have a very interesting explanation for the phenomenon. It simply means there is a possum walking across the very spot you will be buried when you die. Now when you hear someone say, "Oh, a possum just crossed my grave!" you will have a better understanding of a sudden unexplained shiver.

FUNERAL RIBBON QUILT

My husband's mother was an avid reader from the city. She lived for many years in New Jersey; moved to Binghamton, New York, after retirement; and then came to Loveland, Ohio, where I was privileged to be the major part of her care.

One day as we were talking, she shared something she had read in a book about the Appalachian foothills people.

She had read about a woman who saved wide ribbons from funeral flower arrangements, and when she had collected enough, she used them to make a quilt. She was struggling to believe this could be true.

I made no attempt to convince her that this was common practice. I simply pulled my own funeral-arrangement-ribbon quilt top from a drawer to show her.

A picture really is worth a thousand words. Maybe more!

Note: in those days, the ribbons on funeral flower arrangements were made from strips of satin fabric, not synthetic like we mostly see today.

DECORATION DAY

I t wasn't just at funerals and wakes that attention was given to honoring the deceased. Decoration Day, or the "Thirtieth," was the occasion that gave everyone the opportunity to remember the many people who had gone on before them.

The person who passed was not buried one day and forgotten after a few weeks or months. Stories about how they lived, laughed, loved, worked, and dealt with everyday issues were repeated and handed down. As time goes on, things change. I am motivated to write because families are less likely to gather and share the simple stories of every life from past generations.

Aunt Hettie died three years before I was born, but I feel like I knew her because Mom, Grandma, and others kept her memory alive through conversation and shared stories that preserved the image of the kind, loving, and humble person that was Aunt Hettie.

Almost every woman in the community began several weeks before the "Thirtieth" to gather the things needed for making flowers to decorate graves of family and friends. Most were very skilled at creating a beautiful variety of flowers. Throughout the year, no piece of wire was thrown away, for it could be cut and used for wiring the flowers together and for making the stems.

Sometime in early spring, the general store would get in a supply of crepe paper in assorted colors—red, pink, yellow, orange, blue, and green. Days before the holiday, women would greet each other at the store or post office. During this time of year, conversations usually began with, "You got your flares (flowers) made yet?" Most women worked hard every day doing household chores, child-rearing, washing and ironing, performing outside farm work, gardening, and canning. Making the flowers was most often attended to on a rainy day or after all the work was done at the end of the day.

Grandma Crase had a natural ability to grow flowers, and her yard was always colorful and fragrant. Cut flowers from her own garden were sometimes snipped, arranged, and used to decorate the cemeteries. She also sought out wild honeysuckle on the hillsides and incorporated them into arrangements to decorate the graves.

When the day came, we got up early, dressed in our best clothes, and set out for the cemeteries on Wheelrim (a Morgan County tributary off Johnson Fork). We went prepared to spend the entire day, going first to a memorial service on the Elam Cemetery. The goal was to get there early and put the crepe paper flowers on the graves, all before the singing and preaching began.

The service could go on for hours. Every preacher who showed up was given a turn to preach.

When the morning service ended on the Elam Cemetery, family and friends would gather, usually at Emmie and John Henry Crase's home. Most families brought at least one box or basket of food to set "dinner on the ground."

After consuming a satisfying selection of home-cooked dishes and enjoying a time of visiting and playing, everyone set off for the head of Wheelrim, where the events of the morning were repeated on the Crase Cemetery. The singing, praying, and preaching went well into early evening.

These events were always well attended. Most folks who had moved away to another state made an effort to come back home for Decoration Day. It was an important day to remember those who had passed on and also a day to reconnect with friends and family who were still living.

A meal following the June meetin', a memorial service that was held on the hilltop just in front of the house on Red River.

Cousin Charlie Crase, delighted to be riding a horse. Sadly, Charlie passed away in 2019 at age seventy-four. He dealt with cerebral palsy since his birth. Pictured also is Uncle Chester Lovely.

Norma Patrick Seto

THE BLESSING

Cornelius Keeton was a neighbor, friend, farmer, fox hunter, and father of several sons and one daughter. A zealous man, Cornelius was a strong believer who, with God's help, had overcome pitfalls of the flesh and habits of his youth.

In his last years, Cornelius dealt with serious health problems, and it became necessary for doctors to amputate his legs. The amputations did little to improve his situation, and eventually Cornelius became totally bedridden. There was little that could be done to help him. Friends and neighbors kept vigil, waiting with the family for his inevitable demise.

Their house was located at the head of Turkey Branch. They had no electricity and very little light came through the windows of the room in which Cornelius lay dying. Yet I remember being impressed by the whiteness and crispness of the bedsheets.

The weather was very hot, and no breeze came through the window to give comfort. Cornelius had blue eyes that were the color of a spring sky; they were full of pain but mixed with expressions of gratitude as I took my turn fanning him with a piece of cardboard. As the makeshift fan moved the air to cool his brow, he looked into my face and sincerely said, "God bless you."

That prayer uttered from the lips of a dying man impacted my life in positive and profound ways. I was grateful for and recognized the power in the sincere prayer appeal to the Heavenly Father on my behalf. I learned through this experience the value of giving and receiving a prayer blessing, and I do not undermine the value and importance of the words, "God bless you."

I was about eleven years old at the time.

MAN CALLED MARTIN

Few people knew Martin as long or as well as my family knew him. It is said that a man in Martin's early life beat him and stomped him in the head with a peg leg. The injury to Martin from the wooden hand-hewn leg prosthesis left deep depressions on his head and behind his ears and rendered him almost completely deaf.

Martin was never tested to determine how much damage he suffered from that incident. Because of his age at the time, language did not develop for him beyond a few words and grunts. He most certainly learned to read lips. He developed his own way of signing to get a point across. He would sometimes go through motions, using a few words, pause, and then laugh robustly. He had a good sense of humor. Sometimes it took a lot of concentration to understand the joke to be able to laugh with him. Sometimes you just didn't get it at all.

Martin had clear, expressive, and intelligent eyes. He was always clean and well-mannered. He had a very bald head in his final years.

Martin was the product of his mother's marriage prior to her marriage to Gertis Cole, the man who raised Martin and gave him his name. Gertis was a poor man who never seemed to get ahead enough to rise above the poverty level. However, as I recall, he was a gentle man and a good neighbor.

Mom and Dad lived on Settlement Branch when my sister was born. Dad dealt with depression most of his life. He had so much difficulty coping with the possibility of losing Mom in childbirth that he went into a full-blown nervous breakdown. He didn't want anything to "die," including weeds that needed to be cut from crops. That rendered him temporarily ineffective as a farmer. Neighbors rallied to help see the crops to completion that year.

The Cole family lived just across the branch from Mom and Dad. Martin, recognizing Mom was having a difficult time, helped by keeping her well supplied with wood and coal. He also helped with the garden, hoeing and harvesting.

Even during the difficult times, Mom kept up the practice of going to church. It was a long walk out of Settlement Branch and up Johnson Fork to Mount Zion Baptist Church. On Sundays when Dad was not able to accompany her, Martin would show up ready and willing to carry baby Juanita the few miles so Mom didn't have to miss Sunday services.

Many years later, Juanita and I were in the Coffee Cup in Salyersville when Martin walked into the restaurant. He recognized us right away. As he walked toward us, eyes focused on Juanita, he cradled his arms and started swaying back and forth to remind us of the many times so long ago that he had lovingly carried her to church.

I was fourteen years old when Grandpa Crase had a stroke and died from it. Mom, Dad, and Uncle Vencin were called to his side and spent the time on Red River through the process. Martin was there to stay with my sister and me. I remember we made fudge to keep Martin happy. I do not remember if we fed him anything else, but he did not seem disappointed as long as the fudge kept coming.

When Gertis and June started to age, their children began to go out on their own. For many years, Martin wandered from one household to another on Johnson Fork. Most people welcomed him, fed him, and provided a place for him to sleep. He was always free to leave whenever he wanted. Martin was willing to work for his keep and would sometimes be paid for his efforts. Some people took advantage of his willingness to work hard for little or no pay. Because of his lack of understanding about money and the value of his time, he might be satisfied with being paid just fifty cents a day.

It was considered an unlikely event by some, but late in his life,

Martin found love and married Mae. Martin finally was able to experience the joy and comfort of a permanent home and companion.

At some point, because of his disabilities and advancing age, Martin was able to draw Social Security income. He had just received and cashed his check when some young thugs followed him to a remote place on Mine Fork. They mugged him and stole his money and his treasured pocketknives. He was strong, but he was probably an easy target for the hoodlums as they stealthily came up from behind and overpowered him. He didn't do well after the robbery. His confidence was destroyed. He became very much aware of his vulnerability because he couldn't hear.

Sometime later, I came across some pocketknives at a garage sale and bought them for Martin. I intended to take them to Kentucky to give to him, but Martin passed away before I was able to get there.

God rest your soul, Martin. You were a good man and a loyal friend.

I REMEMBER "PRETTY GRANNY"

elilah (Lilly) Lykins was born on March 13, 1865 and died on November 28, 1953. She married Henry Elam (1857–1930). Henry is remembered by his granddaughter Maxine Patrick as a gentle, soft-spoken man who treated everyone with dignity and respect. Henry and Delilah had three daughters; Lucy Belle married Reverend Andy Crase, Emma married Howard Bailey, and Laura married John Bailey. (John and Howard Bailey were brothers.) Those three daughters produced forty-five children: fifteen, fourteen, and sixteen, respectively.

When Henry Elam died, Delilah married Willie Williams. Willie was not so popular with the grandchildren.

When asked why she chose to marry again at her advanced age, Pretty Granny replied to her granddaughter, "An old cat loves cream as well as a kitten."

Lilly was best known to her grandchildren and great-grandchildren as "Purty Granny." She was a very small, very pretty woman.

For many years, Lilly Elam was a competent and reliable midwife for portions of Morgan, Magoffin, Wolfe, and Breathitt Counties. She rode on horseback to deliver babies through all sorts of weather and circumstances. Also known as an herb doctor, she made regular trips into the woods and fields to gather herbs and plants to stock her primitive but effective pharmacy. For difficult labor, she prescribed a tea made from boiled eggshells.

Mom said she was there when Purty Grannie was getting ready to deliver one of Hettie's babies. As it got close to time, Mom (seventeen or eighteen at the time) said she would go to get Aunt Daught to help. Purty Grannie stopped her, saying it was important that Mom learned about such things. The two of them took care of business. Mom said she mostly just handed things to Purty Grannie through the delivery. She was paid from fifty cents up to two dollars for a delivery.

At the end of each day, she enjoyed sitting by a warm fire as she smoked her clay pipe (smoking that pipe was probably her only vice).

Lucy Belle's youngest children, the twins Faye and Raye, remember going to visit Granny and sleeping and playing in big high beds. Faye remembers exploring pockets, purses, drawers, nooks, and crannies when Pretty Granny thought they were taking a nap.

Tasty homemade sweets were always available and freely shared. Faye also remembers that Pretty Granny wore glass beads, clear and black in color, and she carried large black purses. Faye was convinced she carried babies in those purses. She wore string or broom straws in her pierced ears most of the time. She was not above telling a colorful joke or story, and often her daughter Lucy Belle would voice disapproval.

Delilah lived in Adele, Kentucky. Her grandson, Kiser Crase, stayed with her for three years while he went to high school at Canal City during the 1930s.

This story just recently surfaced in Mom's memory when I was asking questions about family. Purty Grannie died in 1953. In those days, families were still opting to bury without embalming, and it was not unusual for the person to be laid to rest in a homemade wooden coffin, and so it was with Purty Grannie. She was laid out in a wooden coffin in the home of her youngest daughter, Laura, in Lee City, Kentucky. It was in the fall, and the weather was warm. The coffin was placed at an open window with just a screen over the opening. It was never acceptable to leave a body unattended between death and burial, so Mom, her sister Savannah, and her cousin Suzie (three granddaughters) were taking a late evening turn keeping vigil. Mom says the conversation, though lively, was kept low and respectful. Suddenly a cat jumped from the outside onto the screen, just behind the coffin, with all four feet and claws firmly attached. The young women were running over each other trying to exit the room. The cat was equally frightened by the hysterical reaction and squalled loudly as it tried to free itself from the screen. Purty Grannie had a sense of humor, and I am sure she would have laughed hysterically at the sight. She may have even orchestrated it!

Willie Williams and Delilah Lykins Elam Williams, midwife and herb doctor.

THE ENTREPRENEUR

A stone chimney stands two stories tall and rises from thick established vegetation that gives no other clue that a cabin once stood on these grounds. No mortar or clay holds the stones in place, and there is no evidence that any was ever used in its construction. Yet it stands tall and straight, flat rocks of varying size and thickness carefully and skillfully placed and fitted to last—a monument to the patriarchal family long since departed.

The man was not only a skilled stonemason; he had also mastered his destiny and his environment by maximizing all his options.

A short walk up the hill and a little searching in the undergrowth reveals a large round grinding stone. At least eight inches thick and four feet across, it was used to grind grain into usable consistency for making bread.

There are still more signs of fruit and vegetable cellars dug into the hillside to hold the produce, which was sold for profit to friends and neighbors. Along the hillside, depressions with earthen sides indicate a number of these caches and substantiate the stories that large quantities of food were grown and stored here to sell when food grew scarce in the community. Most people shared freely, but this was a businessman who was highly motivated to make money. However, he was very reluctant to spend it.

Mom (Maxine) remembers visiting the family's cabin. At the time of her visit, the man's wife had long since passed and of his many children, only two daughters remained at home. Mom was nineteen years old and a new bride. The daughters in the family were older and cordial but shy. They were pleased to see my young mom, who was outgoing and very pretty. When the girls smiled, Mom observed that one had fairly good teeth but the other clearly had many cavities that had been filled with something that could not easily be identified. Mom later learned that their father made a practice of filling the cavities in his family members' teeth with molten lead.

Time passed, and the daughter with dental problems died. No diagnosis was recorded. In those days, if a person died with an ailment from the neck up, the diagnosis was catarrh. Any ailment from the neck down was simply labeled consumption. In the case of this frugal man's daughter, there is a strong possibility that she died from lead poisoning.

At his daughter's death, the man was not forthcoming with the funding for a respectable burial. Knowing him for the tight hold he kept on his money, Grandpa Andy Crase and John Henry Coffey spent twenty-four cents to buy new nails for the purpose of making a suitable coffin. The nails were given in a gesture of support and sympathy. The girl's father went straightaway and returned the new nails for a cash refund, kept the money, and assembled his daughter's coffin using rusty nails he extracted from a fence near his cabin.

Most people took seriously the responsibility of caring for farm animals. Milk cows and work horses were critical to people's livelihood and were deserving of respect and good care.

This man would ask nearby farmers to save cobs after their own farm animals had eaten away the corn. He would then collect the cobs and add salt to entice his own animals to eat the empty cobs. There was little food value in the cobs, but it filled their stomachs and conserved corn in his own crib.

The chimney as it has stood for well over one hundred years.

NORMA PATRICK SETO

THE COMFORT OF SETTLEMENT BRANCH

The walk to Grandma and Grandpa Patrick's house took us across hills and through the woods and eventually brought us to the chipyard at their back door. The chipyard was an area that had been used for wood chopping. Over the years, small chunks of wood chips accumulated to cover the ground. The dry chips could be used as kindling for the fireplaces and cookstove. I remember picking up chips to fill a large bucket. The supply far exceeded the demand, and a bucketful taken from the thick layer that spread over the yard could hardly be noticed.

If we arrived around suppertime, the smell of baking corn bread wafted out the back door and up the holler, hanging sweetly in the air. I knew as we crested the last hill that I'd be enjoying a big slice of hot corn bread and a glass of fresh milk as soon as I stepped through the back door.

My Grandma Patrick's house was the most welcoming place on earth, and I loved being there. Yet it was a home where the kitchen walls were papered with several layers of newspaper and every piece of furniture was strictly functional. With the exception of a few pictures on the walls, no space was used up for things that were purely decorative.

A horseshoe hung over the doorway that led from the front room to the kitchen. It was there for good luck, and Grandpa was careful to make sure the ends pointed upward so the good luck would not spill out.

The house was located at the very head of Settlement Branch, where several hills came together and stopped short of bumping into each other, creating a clearing just big enough for a house and a garden. The barn was situated at the side of the path that led out to the main road. Corn and tobacco were grown in the small bottoms located along the path that led out of the holler.

My cousins, who would visit from Cincinnati, remember stepping outside on a clear night just to enjoy the brilliance of the stars. In this place the night sky could be appreciated and observed without interference from any other light source. It was a spectacular event that could be experienced and remembered at Grandma's house.

On occasion, if company was expected, Grandma would catch one of her chickens, grab it by the neck, and spin it in circles. When it was brought to the point of unlikely recovery, she would release it. To make plucking the feathers easier, the chicken was plunged into boiling water. Once the feathers were plucked, the next step was to singe it with a strip of burning brown paper to burn off the pin feathers. After all that, it was ready to be cut for frying. I don't remember ever feeling timid about the method; it was simply the way it was done.

A few years ago, I was asked to give a short talk at a Mother's Day event at my church. Someone else was asked to talk about mothers, and my speech was to be about grandmothers. I had just become a grandmother myself, and I was excited to tell about how my grandmothers had been such a big part of my life. It was also an opportunity to resurrect and examine the memories that might help to make me a good grandma.

What was it that made me love my Grandma Patrick so much? I can't remember any material gift from her to me, for she did not have the means. Going out to eat was unheard of because there were no restaurants. Grandma seldom ventured into the county seat, so trips were certainly not a thing she would or could have given. What I do know and remember is that she gave her love so completely and unconditionally.

I'll illustrate with a personal memory and continue with a contribution from my sister.

Once the fire in the fireplace went out, our houses got really cold at night. Beds in Grandma's home were piled high with quilts over featherbed or shuck bed mattresses. Because she couldn't be sure we'd stay under all those covers, she slept with my sister and me to make sure we kept warm. I remember waking several times during the night to feel her hand tucking the quilts tightly around us so that no cold air got to us.

My sister reminded me that Grandma Lizzie always allowed us freedom to do what we wanted at her house, especially when it came to cooking. Although her supplies were limited, she never held back or scolded if we used more than we should or if a dish didn't turn out well because it was purely experimental. Both my sister and I have the reputation of being good cooks. For us, the joy of cooking most likely began with days spent at Grandma Patrick's home.

Grandma was a woman full of compassion. She would walk for miles to help someone in need. She was a hardworking woman. She literally worked like a man on their farm, plowing, planting, and harvesting. She milked cows and took care of the chickens and livestock. She once hatched an egg by carrying it in her ample bosom. She loved to go barefoot. She was a large woman.

Grandma Lizzie was second wife to Fairsh. He first married Lula Banks, and to them was born a daughter, Rosie. First wife Lula was leaving a memorial service on a hilltop cemetery. She was probably overdressed in a long skirt, long sleeves, high collar, and hat. A sudden storm came up, and she became soaked by a cold rain. The belief was that she developed pneumonia from that incident and died as a result. Fairsh was left with a two-year-old to raise. In those days, there were no day care options, so he had little or no help. He wasted no time trying to court Lizzie and showed up at her door just days after Lula's funeral.

Grandma Lizzie was interested in him but did not want to entertain any notion of courtship so soon after his wife had passed. She said to him, "Wait until her signs (footprints) get out of the yard and come back." He waited for three weeks and returned. One can only speculate that there was some rain to speed up the process of removing the footprints. They married, raised Rosie together, and had nine more children—Myrtle, Homer, Rebecca, Frances, Freeling, Logan, Gertie, Vencin, and McCoy. Their arrangement was unique for their time in that he did the housework (except for cooking) and she did the outside work.

Lizzie and her sister Cora remembered their grandma talking about Union soldiers coming through, stealing food.

Cora's granddaughter also remembers being told that the same great-grandparent chased away Union soldiers when they tried to raid their home, searching for supplies and confiscating livestock for food.

She tolerated the raiding to a point, but when the soldiers tried to take her dried apples, they experienced the fullness of her wrath. It suddenly became great-great-grandma against the Union Army! She chased them away! There was just too much work involved in preserving those apples to easily give up the fight.

A SPRING DAY TO REMEMBER

everal years ago, I convinced Uncle Vencin to walk the path up
Settlement Branch with the intent of recovering Grandma's old
cupboard.

The design suggests Shaker, although I have no idea of its origin.
It is old; the finish is original, and over time it has developed a
buttermilk paint pattern.

We set out, accompanied by my son Matthew, age ten; his friend,
who was also ten years old; and my daughter Kelly, who was eight
years old. It was a beautiful day to be enjoying the early green foliage
and the cool mountain air.

Spring rains had made for a wet and muddy trek going in and a
near impossible retrieval of the cupboard coming out, but we were
determined to complete the mission. Equipped with a strong rope
and a wheelbarrow, Uncle Vencin and I took turns being the horse
(puller) and the pusher of the wheelbarrow.

We finally made it to the pickup truck after several hours of
pushing and pulling over waterfalls, in and through the creek, and
through slick mud on inclines and declines and thick and sucky mud
on level ground.

The youngsters enjoyed most of the trip, but after a few hours, I
figured this would not go down on their list of pleasant memories.
Imagine my surprise when as a college student, Matt wrote the
following poem describing that day.

He has given me permission to include it with this story.

Lizzie McQuire's Cabinet

She said it may be Shaker
then I knew
and looked down at my boots
caked with mud
From where the Appalachians shouldered in
on beech and briars and brook
that tugged and stuck and soaked
into your skin before they let you pass.
So this is what we're made of
overhanging mossy haunches of hills that never move
shafts of morning sun sinking into greens
glowing gold in maple leaves
deep pools of evergreen needles
black in the shadowed moss and lichens
and rising on the morning brume
no wonder she wants a piece to bring home.
A piece?
I picture kids, maybe three or four
imitating china stacked on sturdy shelves
that can barely contain the giggles
while someone searches
So, with a stubbled rope,
we lashed it like the daughter of the Hesperus
to a stumbling rusted barrow
slogging through the pool with the snake ribbon ripples
down the fall drowning in Spring's deluge
stuck in the sucking clay mud (this is a road?)
and into the sun
past the rock that turns over when it hears the rooster crow
to the pickup driven up Settlement Branch
as far as it would go.

—Matt Seto, January 1993

NORMA PATRICK SETO

*A scene from the front yard of Fairsh and Lizzie
Patrick's home on Settlement Branch.*

GRANDMA'S SMOKEHOUSE

A while back, I took a three-hour hike up Settlement Branch to the old homeplace where Grandma and Grandpa Patrick once lived. The house and outbuildings are now there only in my memory. The smokehouse that sat close behind the main house near the back door has long since been torn down.

The well is there. It has been covered against the possibility that someone might wander by unknowingly and fall into it.

Empty jars and stored food once filled the smokehouse, but all that is left now are shards of pottery and broken glass. Pretty pieces of aqua, blue, clear, and amber glass are strewn over the ground. The pieces are what is left of jars that were once filled with tomatoes, green beans, corn, apples, peaches, huckleberries, gooseberries, blackberries, and more.

I also remember jars filled with homemade sausage rendered and fried in grease just before it went into them. The hot grease was poured over the sausage to the top of the jar just before the jar was sealed. After a short time, the grease would solidify and turn white. The brown sausage visible against the white grease looked so good, but we might now label that a "heart attack preserved in a jar."

I wondered where she might have come by the pottery, which, evidenced by the broken pieces, were part of a beautiful and colorful pattern. I felt fortunate to have found small pieces with pictures of birds and flowers intact. There were also pieces of thick brown crockery wear, what's left of very functional pieces important to preserving, pickling, or sulfuring fruit and vegetables. More shards

Norma Patrick Seto

lay over the ground that looked like pieces of churns, so important to the process of making butter and buttermilk.

I picked up many pieces to save in a vase to remind me of the good things that were kept in Grandma's smokehouse.

THE DAY GRANDPA
WORE A DRESS

Grandpa Fairsh was a man born before his time. He was a good house husband. He made beds, swept floors, emptied chamber pots, and mended all sorts of things, including clothing. He had limited tools, some of them handmade.

I can picture clearly a very primitive homemade awl. It was a piece of wood driven through with a nail so that the sharp end of the nail protruded about an inch and a half past the small carved piece of wood. It was used to punch holes in leather to repair shoes, boots, belts, and saddles.

Grandpa was not big on doing outside work. One day, for a reason not remembered, Grandma was not able to milk the cow. The cow was accustomed to the gentle touch and the soft image of a woman. When Grandpa settled himself on a stool to begin milking, the cow resisted. Grandpa figured out very quickly what the problem was and came up with a solution that got the job done. He went back into the house, put on a dress and bonnet, and returned to the barn to try again. It was just the visual the cow needed. Grandpa got full cooperation from the cow, which resulted in a full bucket of milk.

*Fairsh and Lizzie McQuire Patrick at their home on the main road,
Johnson Fork. Lizzie never got accustomed to living away from the
Settlement Branch house. She developed Alzheimer's disease late in
life, and her desire every single day was to go "back home."*

FLEEING THE FEDS

When he was a young man, Grandpa Patrick took flight out West because he sold a pint of whiskey, got found out by the law, and decided to run before he could be arrested. After he got far to the West, he became so homesick that he decided it was best to return home and pay the penalty. I think he was in jail for a time. He never sold another drop of moonshine.

PUFFING WITH PAPAW

Do you know about rabbit tobacco, better known as life everlasting? Grandpa always said it was good for your health, so Mom would let us smoke it with him. I can still picture it—my white-haired grandpa sitting before the fireplace, smoking that stuff with his little (at the time six-, seven- or eight-year-old) granddaughter. We rolled it in brown paper and licked the edges to hold it in a shape for lighting and smoking.

Life everlasting is a wild plant with straight stems found usually in a cluster of eight or ten shoots. Leaves grow from the base all the way up the stem, ending in a cluster of light yellow flowers at the top. When the leaves are dry enough to harvest, you grasp the stem at the bottom and strip the dry leaves by pulling upward in a single motion. It is not illegal or addictive.

Life everlasting does not taste like tobacco, and it is not hallucinogenic. We suffer no adverse side effects from having shared this unusual pastime with Grandpa. He may have been right; he lived a good long life. Except for hearing loss, he remained healthy throughout. He was never a tobacco smoker and only occasionally and in season did he smoke "life everlasting."

Fairsh Patrick was an honest man and a good man.

I later learned that life everlasting, or rabbit tobacco, is supposedly a good respiratory herb and was used by Native Americans in tea and incense. It was used to treat coughs and colds, as well as asthma and other respiratory ailments. It is antiviral and astringent (helps to tighten up soft tissue, which can be good for the digestive tract and respiratory system).

BUTTON ON THE DOOR

The simplest things will sometimes trigger a pleasant memory or remind me of the way we lived and functioned.

The "button" on a door was not like a button that you'd find on a garment, but it did work to hold something together or closed.

A "button" was simply a piece of wood cut or whittled into the appropriate size and shape for the purpose. It was more utilitarian than decorative.

Oval or rectangular in shape, it was driven through with one nail so it could be turned vertically to allow a door to swing freely. When it was turned horizontally, it worked well to keep a door closed.

Buttons were used on closet doors, outhouses, smokehouses, chicken houses, and corn cribs. If a door swung to the outside of the building, the button was nailed to the casing around the door. If the door opened to the inside, the button was nailed to the door itself.

On occasions when I would be sent to the smokehouse or to the chicken house to gather eggs, without fail, I would be asked, "Did you button that door back?"

PEDDLERS A PLENTY

Most people were self-sufficient when it came to goods and food. Vegetables were planted, harvested, and preserved. Hogs and chickens were raised for food. Sheep were a source of food, but they were also kept for the wool they produced. Grandma Crase sheared, carded, spun, and sometimes dyed to get the wool she used to keep her large family supplied with scarves, socks, and mittens. I remember the spinning wheel that sat on her porch long after she stopped using it. Someone painted it blue, and it is probably still being used as a decorative piece in a relative's home somewhere.

Although many necessities were grown or created by the family, peddlers did a brisk business when they came through on horseback or by wagon to entice the people to buy spreads, rugs, tools, hair fixtures, and combs, just to name a few items.

Peddlers were not necessarily known by locals. Their character and integrity was sometimes uncertain, but hill country hospitality dictated that at the nearest home he would be offered food and lodging at the end of the day. A dry comfortable stall and food for his horse or horses was also usually provided.

On one such occasion, Grandma Patrick took a peddler in to stay the night. Details are not clear, but for some reason she became displeased with him. To show her aggravation, she charged him a dozen eggs for lodging. He never came back.

The Crase family experience with a peddler was similar. Grandpa Crase was a circuit-riding preacher, which kept him away from home a lot. Grandma was capable and confident in his absence, but on one occasion she had reason to question her decision to provide lodging for a peddler. Daughters Eliza and Hettie were near grown and very pretty, and it may have been that the man was inappropriate in word or action. In any case, Grandma was concerned enough that she sent for neighbors Willie M. Davis and Ollie Davis to come stay the night. Grandma put all the children and herself in one room and barred the door while the two friends kept an eye on the peddler.

Mom (Maxine) was about eight years old (she is now one hundred), and she remembers that the man rode a very big horse laden with large packs filled with goods like bedspreads, scarves, etc.

I'm sure that incident made my grandma more careful and discerning about taking in strangers, but it did not stop her from being compassionate and hospitable. She continued to lodge strangers and feed the poor from her own very limited resources.

The next story involves a peddler whose name and origin were not known. He was found shot to death along the wayside. His horse and wares were not found. Since there was no way of identifying him or contacting his family, the local people prepared his body, dug a grave, and Preacher Andy Crase conducted a funeral service. The mystery peddler was buried in an unmarked grave on Wheelrim in the Crase family cemetery. As far as Mom remembers, no authorities were contacted.

Just a few years ago, Walker Crase felt the need to get a marker for the grave. He presented his request to the members of Wheelrim Baptist Church, asking for donations from those who wanted to give. The people responded, and the grave is now marked with a regular tombstone, into which is carved, "Unknown Peddler."

REALLY? YOU WERE A CHICKEN THIEF?

As I grew up in eastern Kentucky, I was feistier, or more "briggedy," than most youngsters my age. I would be considered outgoing or extroverted by today's standards, but it was not necessarily a positive trait for that time and place. Either I was not told or I chose to ignore the adage that "Children should be seen and not heard." Although it may have been a source of grief for my own parents, other adults in the neighborhood found it fun to banter and tease with me. Such was the case with Waymen Tackett. Since I can remember, each time we'd meet, he would greet me with the question, "Stealin' any chickens?" He was a preacher man and probably did not steal chickens, and neither did I, but it became great fun to pretend, invent, and share chicken stealin' methods with him. I wrote the following poem about one of his shared methods.

How to Steal a Chicken on a Cold Night

Don't sneak up on the chicken,
Nor grab him from the rear,
'Cause when he starts to holler,
Maxine will surely hear.
If you grab him with a sack,
The squawks will sound alert,
You'll be pickin' buckshot
From places that will hurt.
Many methods have been tried,
But most don't do it right.
There's only one surefire way
To steal a chicken on a cold night!
I'll tell you how it's done,
As told by Mr. Tackett—
A way that's worked for him for years.
His chicken coop will back it.
First, you build a fire.
Now, get a small flat board real warm.
Walk up to the chicken coop.
Put on your chicken friendly charm.
You ease the board up close
To a fine fat dumplin' kind of chicken.
He's so cold, he'll walk right on.
No hollers, squawks, nor kickin'.
Now, hurry 'fore the board cools off.
That bird is comfy hot.
You'll have chicken for tomorrow,
And she didn't fire a shot.

—Norma Patrick Seto

THE INGENUITY OF A MOUNTAIN WOMAN

Mom was a hundred years old on August 5, 2020. She was born one of fifteen children and married Coy, who was one of ten. The families were close. Most are gone now, and I sometimes wonder how it feels to survive beyond the people who knew you when the important events of life were unfolding and being celebrated. Lonely, I imagine.

That's why I was happy when she reconnected with her old friend and neighbor Fairy Bandy Wilson, who was in her nineties and lived just up the road from me in Morrow, Ohio. Fairy and Mom reminisced on the phone, and I made opportunities for them to visit each other.

I remember hearing a particularly funny story about Fairy when she was a young homemaker living on Settlement Branch on Johnson Fork Road in Magoffin County, Kentucky.

In those days, most everybody in rural Magoffin County rode horseback and usually had more than one good horse or mule for riding or hitching to a sled or wagon when it was necessary to transport more people per horse.

Without exception, every woman owned a churn and dash, and one of the very important family responsibilities was to take care of the milk, which was produced twice daily by the family cows. When the warm milk came into the house from the barn, usually the woman strained the milk through a metal milk strainer lined with a clean piece of cheesecloth. Every kitchen had a nail or a line where the cloth and strainer could be seen after it was washed, rinsed, scalded, and hung to dry after each straining. The milk was then set aside in a cool place, usually in a mountain spring or suspended down the well into the cold, deep water. At some point in the late '40s or early '50s, electricity became available, which made perishable food storage much easier and safer.

Of course, milk that comes directly from the cow is whole milk, and after some time the milk will separate, leaving the cream clearly visible and risen to the top of the clear gallon jars that were used for storing milk.

The cream could then be carefully poured into another container (a churn) and left in a warm place for a few hours to turn, or sour. When the cream was ready for churning, the homemaker put a clean wooden dash through a hole in the lid and down into the churn. She would then choose a comfortable spot where she could socialize with friends or family. In summer, it was nice to enjoy a cool summer breeze on the front porch or in the winter, a spot near the fireplace. The churn dash was most often handmade by a male member of the household using poplar wood that had been carefully selected from the nearby woods.

I remember seeing Aunt Lizie put a dime under her churn to scare away bad spirits and to keep the churn from walking. I've asked others for more information about the tradition/superstition but have found none.

After churning, the contents of the churn miraculously changed to buttermilk (just as appropriately, also called sour milk) with a generous amount of sweet and fluffy butter floating on the top much like clouds.

After the butter was scooped from the top and into a bowl, it was whipped or beaten to remove the excess liquid. Salt was added to taste at some point before the butter started to get more solid.

It is said that Mom's friend Fairy did not like the churning part of this process. She was not willing to give up the twenty or thirty minutes it took, no matter how nice the summer breeze or how pleasant the company. Now, to her great advantage, she had a sharp mind, lots of ingenuity, and a very good trotting mule. She had two gallons of cream, which she distributed evenly into two jars, which she placed in each saddlebag. She then got astride her trotting mule and rode up and down the road until her cream was churned—or trotted—into butter.

Her neighbors Frank and Ruth, Bert and Judy, and also Jim and Lola yelled out a greeting as she rode by, and each family asked her to stop and visit awhile, but Fairy was true to her task. She stayed on that mule until the job was done and she had butter for supper that night.

Sadly, Fairy passed away in 2016 at the age of ninety-nine. I was privileged to share this story at her funeral service.

HAVE A BABY, LEAVE A BABY

This true story is recorded as a memory of Maxine Patrick, who was born in 1920. Her memories of this woman would have started sometime in the mid-1920s. Others remembered and contributed some details. The name of this person has been changed because there is no way to determine who and where her offspring might be and no way to predict how they might react or feel about this being made public.

She tiptoed ever so carefully over mud puddles and small streams to keep her shoes looking new and dirt-free.

Betsy was a unique character and was known for being very pretty, clean, and always well-groomed. She never had a permanent home. She lived off the generosity of families who were willing to provide food and shelter. No payment in goods, money, or services were expected of her, at least none that anyone was willing to talk about.

Mom remembers sharing a bed with Betsy on occasions when she would stop at the Crase home for a night or two when she was en route from one host family to another. Mom and her brothers were very young. Grandpa was a preacher. The stopover provided a safe, neutral, and—by her own choice—very temporary place for Betsy.

Once when Betsy was spotted making her way to the front door, Mom spoke out, saying, "Here comes that old Betsy Eden." Grandma Crase was not judgmental and was always compassionate and hospitable. She reprimanded her daughter for the harsh words and once again welcomed Betsy to share a meal and lodging.

Betsy moved around until she found a family that suited her. She would then settle herself in to stay the few months that became the pattern for her very unusual lifestyle.

After a few weeks with a given family, Betsy would seem to put on weight. It might be assumed that it was due to good cooking and care provided by the host housewife. Pretty soon it would become apparent (but still never discussed) that the expanding waistline was something else entirely: Betsy was pregnant. She remained with the family until a baby was delivered, and then she departed, leaving the housewife to raise a baby that was sired by a male member of her own household.

Betsy would move on to another family, and the pattern would be repeated and continued for the duration of her childbearing years.

Betsy did not carry a tote or a suitcase. She seemed to function with just the clothes on her back. It is remembered that she carried a pouch that held a small amount of flour that she used to powder her face. Also in the pouch were scraps of red crepe paper, which when moistened were used to add color to her cheeks and lips.

Betsy never married, and she never took on the responsibility or claimed any of the children she bore. As old age set in, she found herself very much alone and ended up spending her final days in a home for the poor, also known in those days as the poorhouse.

LIKE A HEN WITH AN EGG BROKE IN HER

Life was difficult for women, who rose before daybreak and usually worked until bedtime. Tending children; planting and maintaining gardens; cleaning house and outbuildings; feeding, milking, and caring for farm animals; washing and ironing; preserving food for winter; making quilts and clothing—these were some of the tasks they were expected to perform. If, after all this, they were in a less than cheerful mood, it might be said of them, "She is going around like a hen with an egg broke in her."

Sometimes a hen would suffer an injury that could cause a fully developed egg to break inside her just before she had a chance to lay it properly. When this happened, the hen would go around in a bad way (mood) for days before she eventually died from it.

THE DAY THE MUSIC DIED

The sun rose over the hilltops and filtered through the light fog and mist that typically lingers in the valley in early morning. I sat on the porch, sipping my way through a steaming cup of coffee, enjoying the sounds of birds chirping as they flitted around in search of food for their young. I found myself remembering and listening for the familiar sound of Mosie as he rode his mule for so many years, delivering mail.

Mosie Walters was one of the last mule-carrying mailmen in this country. Through rain, sweltering heat, snow, and wind, Mosie carried the letters and packages that kept the people in eastern Kentucky connected with family and friends who had relocated to the big city.

Mosie stopped at the small rural post offices of Stella, Kentucky, on Cow Creek; Kernie, at the mouth of Cow Creek; Hager, at the mouth of Turkey Branch and ended at Epson, Kentucky, at the mouth of Long Branch. At each stop, Mosie would leave the mail that had seemingly miraculously made its way from a post office in a large metropolitan area to the small post offices, which were simply four-by-four-foot or four-by-six-foot spots set aside in a family dwelling or a general store. The mail was directed to the addressee using only the person's name and, in our case, Hager, Kentucky. No route number, street address, or zip code was required.

Some families picked up the mail from the post office after Mosie made his daily stop. Others had a mailbox by the side of the route, and Mosie would leave mail in their boxes as he rode by. He or the postmaster would sort that mail before he mounted his mule.

Once sorted, it was put into color-coded "pokes." The pokes had large loops that fit around Mosie's neck. He delivered mail from the pokes to several families along his route.

Mail that was taken out or being delivered to the next post office was carried in saddlebags or large gray bags slung over the mule's back.

Without fail, Monday through Saturday one could hear Mosie singing as he rode his mule up Johnson Fork to deliver the mail. The sound increased in volume and clarity as he made his way up the dusty graveled road that ran from the mouth of Johnson Fork at Route 460 and past the front of our house.

One of his favorite songs was "Golden Slippers," and the youngsters around enjoyed hearing him sing it. I remember calling out to him and hearing other children call out to him, "Sing Slippers, Mose." He would break into song, but not before he paused to pronounce a blessing on the child or children making the request. Mosie loved children. The blessing rings in my head to this day. I take it very seriously and feel the love all over again as I remember his words: "God bless you, little children."

Mosie also sang in church. Reverend Forest Bailey held Sunday service in the Turkey Branch schoolhouse. I enjoyed Forest Bailey's preaching and would attend sometimes by myself, favoring his style over the church that my mom and dad attended.

At the beginning of service, Forest would invite anyone who wanted to participate to come to the front to sing. Mosie was always one of the first to move forward. On one occasion, I remember clearly the singing was well underway—beautiful and inspiring as usual—when all of a sudden Mosie stopped singing, put his foot on a school desk, rolled his pant leg up, and quickly moved his fingers to catch what I assume was a flea. Once the little critter was squashed, Mosie rolled his britches leg down, picked up the song book, and resumed worship in song.

Eventually, Mosie grew too old to get on the mule to deliver mail. His old bones could no longer take the extreme cold and heat.

When Mosie's life ended at a ripe old age, some of the music died also on that day.

However, I know in my heart that Mosie is and has been singing God's praise in heaven. He lived his life in preparation of going there, where there are … most likely … no fleas.

Note: Mosie had a very difficult childhood. His mother died when he was twelve, and shortly after her death, Mosie's father abandoned the family, leaving his six children to fend for themselves. Mosie loved reading and learning. He went to school, but for the most part he educated himself in the classics, mathematics, history, and music. He prepared himself for the teacher's exam, passed it, and taught for one year in a rural Magoffin County school.

MARKING A BABY

I t was believed by many people that any visual or emotional trauma that a pregnant woman might witness or experience could "mark" her baby. For that reason, a woman would avoid anything that had the potential to "mark" her baby. For example, seeing a pig or hog in distress or bleeding could cause your baby to be born with features resembling that of a pig. Seeing blood might cause a baby to be born with an unsightly red birthmark.

Mom did not give this belief any credence and neither did my grandmother and great-grandmother. However, Dad did believe it, and he protected Mom from any out of the ordinary event for fear it would cause a problem.

BABIES AND BELLYBANDS

Bellybands were widths of cloth wrapped around a baby at his or her midsection to protect the umbilical cord and keep it from moving. It was thought that the cord, if not secured and bound snugly, would cause pain for the baby and would also open possibilities for premature detachment.

Bellybands could be purchased or handmade, and it was common practice to use them as late as the 1940s and early 1950s. Mom, out of necessity, made the ones she used for my sister and me. She cut a simple four-by-six-inch strip of cloth and attached strings to each end so the band could be tied securely around the waist and over the belly button.

My sister showed signs that her belly button was going to be an "outie." It was recommended by the local midwife that a silver dollar be placed over the belly button in hopes that added pressure would encourage an "innie." When I asked if the silver dollar was placed directly on the skin, Mom replied, "No. I used a small burnt cloth between the naval and the band." Well, of course my next question was about the burnt cloth. She ironed the small cloth until it was scorched looking. This gave her confidence that it was germ free and safe to place on baby Juanita.

When it became apparent after a time that the silver dollar wasn't making a difference, Mom came up with the idea on her own to replace the coin with a marble. She continued to use the band with the marble until my sister was about a year old.

Thanks to Mom's ingenuity and invention, my sister ended up with a fairly normal looking "innie." She said that did not mean you would be seeing her in a bikini any time soon.

Sadly, my dear sister, Juanita, passed away on May 24, 2018 after this short story was written.

MESSAGE ON A MOTH

I went to live in Cincinnati right after graduating high school. Because I was only sixteen years old, the only job I could get was behind a soda fountain at G.C. Murphy Co. I went to work at Sears as soon as I reached seventeen, which was the age requirement to work there. Minimum age for employment at General Electric was eighteen, and on my eighteenth birthday, I became a GE employee.

For eight years I worked and went to the University of Cincinnati in the evenings.

Eventually I married and had three wonderful children.

I telephoned Mom regularly during those years. She was widowed at age fifty-one, and it was good for both of us to have a Sunday afternoon phone chat.

On one occasion, we were ready to hang up after having covered the news in each of our lives. Mom suddenly said, "Oh, I have something else to tell you. The neatest thing happened to me this morning."

She went on to say that she had been waiting on the porch for someone to pick her up for church. She said she looked down to see something shiny at her feet. Upon closer examination, she discovered it was a moth, and on its back was the shiny white shape of a cross. Looking even closer, she saw the shape of a man on the cross. She said it made her feel so good, she felt the Lord was trying to tell her something. I was taken up in the story and agreed that this was really special. I then asked, "What did you do with it?"

Loudly and without hesitation she replied, "I killed it!"

My immediate thought was that if the Lord was trying to tell her something, she might have shot the messenger! Her reasoning was that she wanted to have it to show at church, and she wanted to save it to show to me on the next visit. That is why she just very carefully "stepped on its little head."

Sure enough, on my next visit, she presented a small box with a clear plastic lid. Resting on a layer of cotton was the moth, just as she had described it. I'm still wondering what the message might have been.

THE BUTTON JAR

We always had a button jar, which was kept against the day when a button was needed to replace one that was lost.

Worn out articles of clothing were not ever thrown away or used for rags before the buttons were removed and added to the collection of buttons in the jar, which was usually a quart mason jar. No found button was ever discarded.

Mom started saving buttons very early in her life and continued to do so over the years as she raised her family. I sense that older family members contributed to ensure that the new young homemaker started off with a good supply of buttons. Mom has pointed out buttons that her sister Hettie gave her and also ones that Grandma provided. As a matter of fact, I still have some of those buttons that she kept in the jar for almost eighty years.

I was inspired to write the following poem when my niece came for a visit and announced straightaway that she had lost a button off her blouse. Of course, I went right for the button jar and started the search for a match. She got the benefit of hearing the history of the button jar and also the origin of some of the buttons. She seemed to enjoy the stories. At that point, I decided to write the following poem, and I began and continued collecting hundreds of buttons over the next few months. At Christmas, each of my wonderful nieces and nephews got a copy of the poem and a mason jar filled with colorful buttons of all sizes and shapes.

NORMA PATRICK SETO

A Family of Buttons in a Jar

A button from a coat that Mamaw wore
And one from your mom's old pinafore
There's one off your uncle's flannel shirt
Another from sister's poodle skirt
Great aunt's button is big and round
And the emerald green was the best one found
Dad popped one as he worked on the plow
And another when he sat to milk the cow
Some more were found in an old used purse
Took one from my sleeve to make this verse
Baby's from clothes that grew too small
Throw 'em in the jar but that's not all
Cousin lost a button while cleaning stalls
Another came from Papaw's old overalls
Storekeep popped one 'cause business was good
And another from a traveler in the neighborhood
All these buttons found around and about
Or clipped from garments that were all worn out
Kept over the years and we've succeeded
To have the right button when one is needed
So when you lose a button from what you wore
No need to go running to the button store
There's no cause to go searching near and far
'Cause we have these buttons in the button jar
There are yellow ones, red ones, tan and blue
These buttons have a history and a story too
And it's not just buttons—there's more by far
It's a family of buttons saved here in a jar.

—Norma Seto

APPENDIX

Medicine

These home remedies and medicinal methods are shared here simply as a historical record and not to be considered as recommendations or interpreted as medical advice.

Aloe plant—For burns.

Blood root—To thin blood.

Boiled poke root—To stop diarrhea in baby chicks, two to three spoons per gallon water.

Burned whisky—For stomachache.

Chimney soot—Use soot to stop bleeding.

Cigarette smoke—Blown in the ear to relieve pain.

Cow manure—Use as poultice for injured hand.

Double-bladed ax—To cut pain, let blood flow or drip onto a double-bladed ax and bury the ax where blood hit the ground.

Eggshell tea—Boil eggshells, strain, and administer the tea to a woman in labor to relieve the pain.

Fat meat—Use as a poultice over a boil.

Goose poop—Boil and strain. Drop into ear for earache.

Honey—For sores.

Hot needle—Running through a wart as close to the base as possible will cause the wart to disappear.

Human urine—Boil and drop in ear for earache.

Jewel weed—For poison ivy.

Kerosene—A drop or two of kerosene in sugar will cure worms.

Mullen leaves—Good for a cough. Boil leaves with sugar until syrupy.

Mullen leaves, pennyroyal, fever weed, and willow—Boil together. Good for a cough. Add a little whiskey to keep the mixture from souring.

Oatmeal—Use as a poultice to draw out boils

Poke Root—Boil poke root and bathe in it for treatment of the seven-year itch. Can add sulfur.

Pregnant mare urine—For treatment of kidney stones.

Queen in the meadow—Brew as tea for kidney and bladder issues.

Sow bugs boiled—Boil and strain bugs. Administer two to three teaspoons at a time to cure a baby with bole hives.

Sassafras—Sassafras tea is a good blood thinner.

Spice wood tea—Boil tender limbs and sweeten with molasses. For comfort.

Squirrel and gravy—For sickness (comfort food like chicken soup, the Appalachian equivalent to a Jewish mama's chicken soup).

Sweet tobacco—For toothache (Brown Mule).

Tobacco poultice—For sting.

Tomato vines—Good for bee stings.

Toothpaste—For burns.

Turpentine—A drop or two of turpentine mixed with sugar will cure worms.

Warm blood of a black chicken—For the treatment of shingles.

Yellow root—Chew yellow root for stomach problems.

Glossary of Terms and Other Explanations

Branch—The stream of water that flows down a hollow (holler). The word *branch* is also interchangeable with holler: "up the branch" or "up the holler." It's the same for creek or river.

Briggedy—Feisty, high energy.

Chamber lye—Boiled down human urine, commonly used to treat earache.

Comb got red—It might be said of a man who is looking for a woman (comparing him to a rooster whose comb will get red when he is looking for a hen).

Dinner on the ground—Makeshift tables on the ground. Planks and stumps were arranged if the meal was spread on the cemetery.

Most of the time, a family would spread their food at the home of a relative who lived closest to the cemetery. If you are not Appalachian, you might say, "Dinner on the grounds."

Ears—Handles on a cooking pot.

Foot log—Footbridge.

Hind parts before—Backward, as in "She has her dress on hind parts before."

Horse-trader—An all-inclusive term for a person who barters and trades.

Laid a corpse—The time before burial when a person has been prepared or laid out for family and friends to hold vigil, which might last sometimes for two or three days.

Nussin'—Simply holding a baby or young child.

On the creek—Where a creek runs the length of the valley. For example, "That is the best person on the creek" would be the same as saying, "That is the best person in the neighborhood."

Out of pocket—Not being where one is supposed to be. Unavailable.

Plime blank—Exactly, as in "She looks plime blank like her mother."

Plunder—Furniture and household items.

Polecat or wood pussy (as in pussy cat)— skunk

Proach—The lane or approach leading up to the house.

Purties—Toys and games, things for play or the entertainment of children. Never did I hear the word *toys* as it related to playthings. Always *purties*.

Rough as a cob—An unrefined person.

Slick as a minner's (minnow's) tail—Devious, conniving.

Slop jar—Chamber pot. Usually one sat near or under each bed in the house. Used instead of going to the outhouse on dark and/ or cold nights.

Sparkin'—Dating, going together.

Sproutin'—Clearing a hillside of trees and briars to create a field for planting or pasture.

Struck on—Sweet on, has a crush.

Thrush doctor—Someone who is born after the death of his or her father.

Turn—Personality. As in, "She has a good turn."

Winderlights—Windows. Honestly, that is the only word I ever heard used for windows until I was about seven years old.

More Sayings and Expression from the Hills.

Interesting to note: Some bad words were called "blackyard words," not to be identified as cuss words. Using God's name in vain was never acceptable. Someone (like my mom) who uses blackyard words very liberally is highly offended when she is accused of cussing. I am guessing that the word *blackyard* is a corruption of the word *blackguard* (a person who uses foul or abusive language).

Beauty is skin deep, but ugly goes all the way to the bone.

Born in the middle of the week looking both ways for Sunday—Ugly or cross-eyed.

Bust your taller box—I will give you a solid whipping. Tallow is a form of rendered fat. Once suet is rendered, it becomes tallow. As long as it is stored in an airtight container (in a small wooden box with a lid) in a cool environment, it can keep for an extended period of time.

Cold as clabber—Pretty cold, referring to food or drink.

Crooked as a dog's hind leg—Usually referring to poor quilting or stitching or a dishonest. person.

Don't that beat the cats afightin'—Frustration at having drawn a bad hand at cards.

Green apple quick steps—The need to hurry to the toilet after having eaten too many green apples.

Head like a cut worm—A person who is very smart.

I'll bust your floater—I will give you a good whipping to bring you back to reality.

My dogs are barkin'—I'm hungry.

Scat, Tom, your tail's in the gravy—What is said when someone sneezes, usually a child. Used in place of "gesundheit" or "bless you."

Skinny as a bean pole—Pretty skinny.

Tough as a hog's nose—A rugged individual.

Walkin' around like she's got an egg broke in her—This would sometimes happen to a hen, which caused the hen to mope around and eventually die.

Ugly as homemade soap—Pretty ugly.

Superstitions

To trim a baby's nails on Sunday will cause her or him to become a thief.

Itching of the right palm suggests you will shake hands with a fool.

A left palm itch means money will cross your palm.

An itchy nose means company's coming.

Ringing in the ears means someone is thinking of you.

AFTERWORD

For several years, I have been working to record family stories. I've written for my own enjoyment and also to preserve the information for my children and grandchildren. Over the last few years, my granddaughter has asked to borrow the stories at least four times, confirming for me that the effort is worth it.

Motivation to get serious about publishing came when Mom said she would like to see the stories in print before she leaves this world. Her memories constitute a large part of the writings in this book and come from her firsthand experience growing up in a large family whose patriarch was a circuit-riding United Baptist preacher. She turned one hundred years old on August 5, 2020.

There are more stories to be told. Please respond with your thoughts on what you have read to give me feedback as to whether you would like to read more. My email address is comax@fuse.net.

Through her heartwarming, humorous, and entertaining memoir of growing up in the hills of eastern Kentucky, Norma invites us to meet colorful characters who lived life the way it was meant to be lived – simply and to the fullest.

—Dr. Jeffrey F. Neal, Director, Cooperative Education Program,
Clemson University, Center for Career and Professional Development,
Suite 316 Hendrix Center, 864.656.3150

Printed in the United States
By Bookmasters